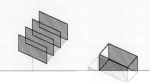

CHINA
HOMEGROWN

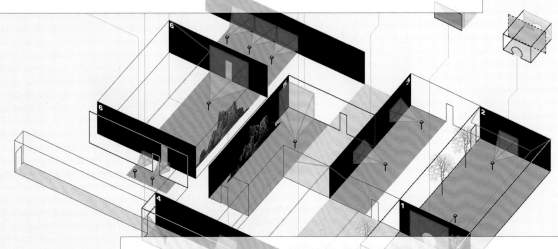

CHINESE EXPERIMENTAL
ARCHITECTURE REBORN

ARCHITECTURAL
DESIGN

November/December 2018
Profile No 256

About the Guest-Editors

Andong Lu and Pingping Dou

05

Introduction
Responsive Experimentalism

Andong Lu and Pingping Dou

06

Integrating Geometry Within a Poetic Setting

Steering a Path Between the Artificial and the Natural

Xinggang Li

16

Arcadia

A Contemporary Chinese Garden Experiment

Xin Wang and Qiuye Jin

24

Lost and Found

Reinventing Multi-Screen Adaptable Architecture

Pingping Dou

32

Constructing Critically

Prefabricated Systems with Soul

Jingxiang Zhu

40

Atelier Li Xinggang, 'Miniature Beijing' – conversion of No 28 Dayuan Hutong, Beijing, 2017

Plugin Society

Bridging the Gap Between Top-Down and Bottom-Up Approaches to Urban Development

James Shen

46

Everyday Change and the Unrecognisable System

Xiahong Hua and Shen Zhuang

52

Informal Density

Animating Historical Neighbourhoods

Hui Wang

58

Atelier Archmixing, Longhua Elder Care Center, Xuhui District, Shanghai, 2016

A New Protocol for Space Production

Generating Socially Cohesive Urban Architecture

Shuo Wang

66

ISSN 0003-8504
ISBN 978 1119 375951

Three Main Drivers of Sustainable Design

A New Architectural Vernacular for China

Yehao Song

74

Wang Zhan,
Artificial Rock No 85,
2005

Basic Green Building Design

Reconnecting Sustainability to the Vernacular

Xiao Fu and Wei You

80

Responsive Structure

Architecture as a Thing-scape

Yichun Liu

88

From Theory to Praxis

Digital Tools and the New Architectural Authorship

Philip F Yuan and Xiang Wang

94

Lighting-Led Architecture

A Collaborative Approach

Xin Zhang

102

Architecture as Synthetic Agency

Narrative-Augmented Design in Practice

Andong Lu

110

Imagining the Immediate Present

Responsive Approaches to the Investigation of Things

Pingping Dou, Andong Lu and Lu Feng

116

Secluded Pavilion of Parasol Tree and Bamboo, Humble Administrator's Garden, Suzhou, 1870s

Turning East

Design Research in China in a Global Context

Murray Fraser

124

Counterpoint

Alternative Modernity, Rural Rediscovery and What Next

The Ongoing Debate on the Modern in China

Li Zhang

134

Contributors

142

Editorial Offices
John Wiley & Sons
9600 Garsington Road
Oxford
OX4 2DQ

T +44 (0)1865 776868

Consultant Editor
Helen Castle

Managing Editor
Caroline Ellerby
Caroline Ellerby Publishing

Freelance Contributing Editor
Abigail Grater

Publisher
Paul Sayer

Art Direction + Design
CHK Design:
Christian Küsters

Production Editor
Elizabeth Gongde

Prepress
Artmedia, London

Printed in Italy by Printer
Trento Srl

Front cover: Archi-Union
Architects, In-Bamboo
community cultural
centre, Chongzhou,
Chengdu, Sichuan
province, 2017. © Li Han

Inside front cover: Li Hua
/TAO (Trace Architecture
Office), Split Courtyard
House, Hutong near
White Pagoda Temple,
Beijing, 2015. ©T-A-O/
Trace Architecture Office

Page 1: LanD Studio,
'Instant Garden'
exhibition, Nanjing Folk
Museum, Nanjing, 2017.
© LanD Studio

06/2018

△D ARCHITECTURAL DESIGN

September/October

2018

Profile No.

256

Disclaimer
The Publisher and Editors cannot be held responsible
for errors or any consequences arising from the use
of information contained in this journal; the views and
opinions expressed do not necessarily reflect those of
the Publisher and Editors, neither does the publication
of advertisements constitute any endorsement by
the Publisher and Editors of the products advertised.

Journal Customer Services
For ordering information,
claims and any enquiry
concerning your journal
subscription please go to
www.wileycustomerhelp
.com/ask or contact your
nearest office.

Americas
E: cs-journals@wiley.com
T: +1 781 388 8598 or
+1 800 835 6770 (toll free
in the USA & Canada)

**Europe, Middle East
and Africa**
E: cs-journals@wiley.com
T: +44 (0)1865 778315

Asia Pacific
E: cs-journals@wiley.com
T: +65 6511 8000

Japan (for Japanese-
speaking support)
E: cs-japan@wiley.com
T: +65 6511 8010 or 005 316
50 480 (toll-free)

Visit our Online Customer
Help available in 7 languages
at www.wileycustomerhelp
.com/ask

Print ISSN: 0003-8504
Online ISSN: 1554-2769

Prices are for six issues
and include postage and
handling charges. Individual-
rate subscriptions must be
paid by personal cheque or
crcdit card. Individual-rate
subscriptions may not be
resold or used as library
copies.

All prices are subject to
change without notice.

Identification Statement
Periodicals Postage paid
at Rahway, NJ 07065.
Air freight and mailing in
the USA by Mercury Media
Processing, 1850 Elizabeth
Avenue, Suite C, Rahway,
NJ 07065, USA.

USA Postmaster
Please send address changes
to *Architectural Design*,
John Wiley & Sons Inc.,
c/o The Sheridan Press,
PO Box 465, Hanover,
PA 17331, USA

Rights and Permissions
Requests to the Publisher
should be addressed to:
Permissions Department
John Wiley & Sons Ltd
The Atrium
Southern Gate
Chichester
West Sussex PO19 8SQ
UK

F: +44 (0)1243 770 620
E: Permissions@wiley.com

Subscribe to △D
△D is published bimonthly
and is available to purchase
on both a subscription basis
and as individual volumes
at the following prices.

Prices
Individual copies:
£29.99 / US$45.00
Individual issues on
△D App for iPad:
£9.99 / US$13.99
Mailing fees for print
may apply

Annual Subscription Rates
Student: £90 / US$137
print only
Personal: £136 / US$215
print and iPad access
Institutional: £310 / US$580
print or online
Institutional: £388 / US$725
combined print and online
6-issue subscription on
△D App for iPad: £44.99 /
US$64.99

Andong Lu
and
Pingping Dou

Andong Lu and Pingping Dou share a common interest in design as investigation and in participatory practice. They are actively involved in research-based studio teaching, nationally funded research projects and educational reform in China, with a focus on experimental design practices. They have also curated a number of exhibitions and their work has been widely published. They received their PhDs from the University of Cambridge and carried out architectural research in the UK before jointly returning to China in 2012 to co-found LanD Studio for Design Research. Based in Nanjing, LanD is a leading design think-tank with multiple roles: an observatory for Chinese urbanism, a centre for innovative research and a laboratory for design experimentation. The studio has successfully conducted six Forums on Design Thinking, the Gewu Workshop (Nanjing, 2015 – see pp 116–23) and the Memory Project of the Nanjing Yangtze Bridge (2014–18 – p 115).

Andong Lu received his BArch from Tsinghua University in Beijing, and MPhil in Architecture and the Moving Image from the University of Cambridge where he also completed his PhD in Architecture in 2009, and was elected a Fellow of Wolfson College in 2010. He is now Chair Professor in Urban Design at the School of Architecture and Urban Planning, Nanjing University, where he additionally acts as director of the Communicable City Laboratory, and also of the Interdisciplinary Centre of Urban Studies at the university's Institute for Advanced Studies in Humanities and Social Sciences. He is a standing member of the Committee of Urban Design, Committee of Architectural Critics and Committee of Architectural Media of the Architectural Society of China. He was previously a guest professor at the Dessau Institute of Architecture, ATCH (Architecture, Theory, Criticism, History) Research Fellow at the University of Queensland, and Henry Luce Foundation Visiting Professor at Pennsylvania State University. His research focuses on urban narratives and place-making, the application of digital media in architecture, and history and theory of modern architecture and urbanism in China. He has guest-edited nine special issues for major architectural journals in China, including the *Architectural Journal*, *Time+Architecture* and *The Architect*. He is also co-editor, with François Penz, of *Urban Cinematics: Understanding Urban Phenomena Through the Moving Image* (University of Chicago Press, 2012) and, with Wowo Ding and Arie Graafland, *Cities in Transition: Power, Environment, Society* (NAi010 Press, 2015).

Pingping Dou received her BArch from Southeast University in Nanjing, and MPhil in Environmental Design in Architecture from the University of Cambridge. She practised at RMJM Architects in London before completing her PhD at the university's Martin Centre for Architectural and Urban Studies. She was then appointed Associate Professor at the School of Architecture and Urban Planning, Nanjing University, and also Visiting Teaching Fellow at Sheffield University in the UK (2016–18). She leads several research grants on morphological optimisation based on multi-agents, environmental performance and urban adaptability. She is currently a guest-editor of www.gooood.cn, the most visited online architectural medium in China, and associate editor of the *Cambridge Journal of China Studies*. She has been published extensively in academic journals and is the author of *World Sustainable Construction* (China Architecture & Building Press, 2008) and *Technology, Humanism and the Cambridge Approach* (Nanjing University Press, 2018).

Responsive Experi

INTRODUCTION

ANDONG LU AND PINGPING DOU

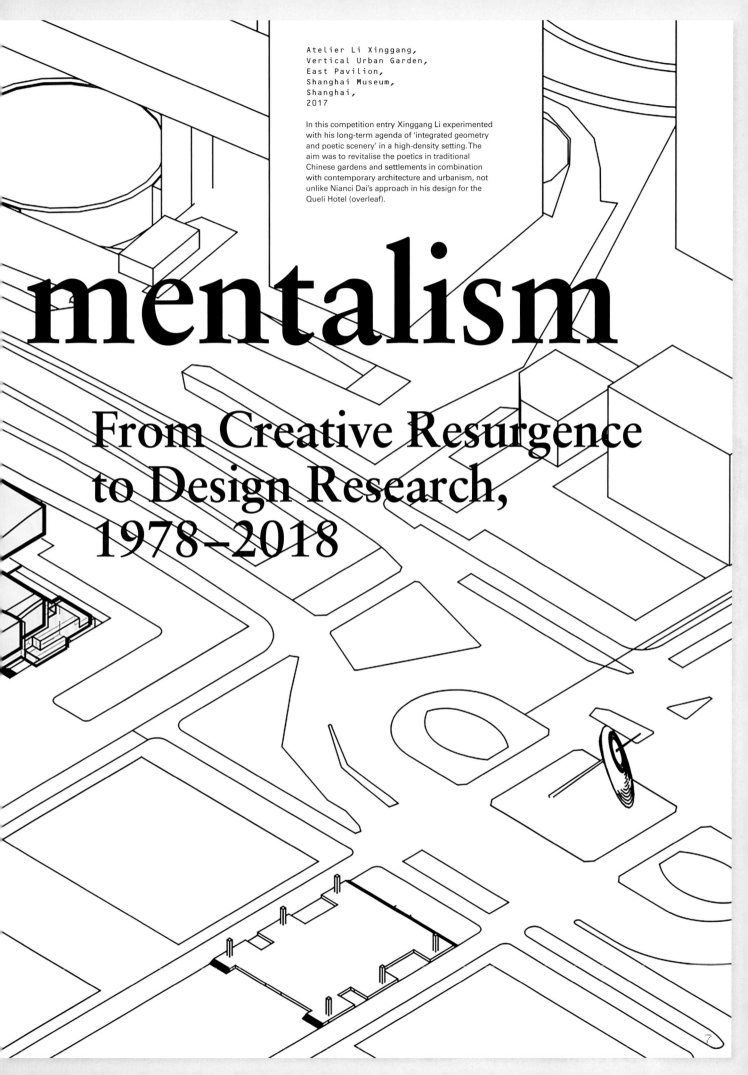

Atelier Li Xinggang,
Vertical Urban Garden,
East Pavilion,
Shanghai Museum,
Shanghai,
2017

In this competition entry Xinggang Li experimented
with his long-term agenda of 'integrated geometry
and poetic scenery' in a high-density setting. The
aim was to revitalise the poetics in traditional
Chinese gardens and settlements in combination
with contemporary architecture and urbanism, not
unlike Nianci Dai's approach in his design for the
Queli Hotel (overleaf).

mentalism

From Creative Resurgence to Design Research, 1978–2018

After the end of the Cultural Revolution, the resurgence of the Committee of Architectural Creation of the Architectural Society of China on 22 October 1978 was a clear signal of the revival of architecture as a creative discipline. In the following years, 'creation' quickly became the predominant keyword to describe the practice of architecture as an art form. In the previous decade of turmoil (1966–1976), the term had been rejected, and educational institutions, professional societies and journals prohibited. As a profession, architecture was instead affiliated with engineering, and architects became engineers. In this context, the architectural renaissance of the early 1980s involved both a fundamental shift in ideas and a comprehensive reformulation of the profession.

Cover of the January
1986 issue of the
Architectural Journal
featuring Nianci Dai's
Queli Hotel,
Qufu, Shandong
province,
1985

In a colloquium on the design of the hotel, Nianci Dai, an eminent architect and national vice-minister, outlined the issues the project sought to address, namely the construction of a new building in a historical environment, and the creation of a traditional Chinese architectural form in relation to modern requirements, modern science and technology.

A Message from Nowhere (1978–91)

The revival of creativity was epitomised by a burgeoning of professional journals within just a few years. These included *The Architect* (1979), *World Architecture* (1980), *New Architecture* (1983) and *Time+Architecture* (1984) – all of which remain key players in Chinese architectural media today. At the same time, conferences and seminars attended by officials, professionals and professors were held to disseminate the ideas of key projects, such as IM Pei's Fragrant Hill Hotel (1982) outside Beijing and Nianci Dai's Queli Hotel (1985) in Qufu, Shandong province, which triggered wide discussion. Requiring cultural expression combined with modern facilities, it was no coincidence that major hotels for international tourists such as these became the primary building type for design experimentation and were at the centre of architectural debate in the 1980s. Among the mainstream profession, attempts to adapt traditional forms to contemporary needs thus became exemplary. However, a peripheral profession was quietly evolving. Design competitions, a new but popular trend, were crucial for a new generation of young architects to advance their ideas via 'paper architecture' at a time when independent practice was not permitted. Many launched their careers through the publication of their award-winning entries in international competitions, among them visionary architects Zaiyuan Zhang, Yung Ho Chang and Hua Tang, who would go on to lead the way in Chinese experimental architecture of the next decade.

This 'Age of New Enlightenment' represented a period of economic reform and social liberalisation in China in which the agendas of modernisation, humanism and the revival of tradition were intertwined to break free from ideological strictures. In architecture, international theories flooded in, creating a complex intellectual landscape. Meanwhile, Postmodernism was hailed with popular enthusiasm and quickly associated with commercial culture and Chinese tradition. It was against this complicated backdrop that the so-called 'experimental architecture' emerged.

Usage of the words 'creation' (blue line) and
'research' (red line) in titles of articles in
the *Architectural Journal*,
1977-2017

Established in 1954 as the journal of the Architectural Society of China, the *Architectural Journal* was the only professional periodical in China until 1979 and is still the most recognised and subscribed to today.

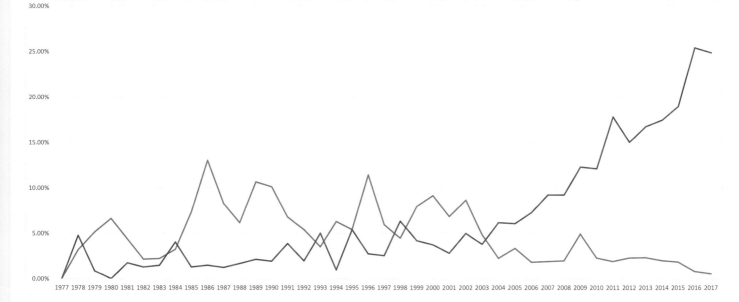

Back to Basics (1992–9)

During his legendary 'southern tour' in 1992, then Chinese leader Deng Xiaoping urged for a quicker transition into a market economy and more aggressive economic development. This soon boosted an upsurge in real-estate and large-scale privatisation that transformed Chinese architecture in the 1990s. Rapid and uncontrolled urbanisation and the iconography of commercial culture stimulated self-conscious resistance to imported architectural notions and styles and a growing sentiment that contemporary Chinese architecture could only come from personal reflection of cultural traditions and urban reality. On the other hand, the lifting of the regulatory barrier to private practice, first in Shenzhen and Guangzhou in 1993 and then in all major cities in 1995, soon instigated the emergence of 'independent architects' as counterparts to those working within state-owned architectural design institutes.

The early years of the decade witnessed increasing resistance among this peripheral group of visionary architects to both kitsch commercial architecture and mainstream academia. Though this sentiment of resistance had arisen earlier, in the mid- to late 1980s, partly inspired by the '85 New Wave' avant-garde art movement, a common agenda of 'experimental architecture' among this small

coterie would not be formulated until the mid-1990s when these young practitioners began using exhibitions and publications to propagate their ideas and to influence architectural discourse. Hua Tang, for example, was the first Chinese architect to hold a solo exhibition, in 1993; while Yung Ho Chang established the first private architectural firm, Atelier FCJZ, in 1996 after 11 years of teaching in the US, and the following year published *Feichang Architecture* (literally, 'unusual architecture'), a biographical monograph of his visionary design projects since the mid-1980s that demonstrated his enthusiasm for reinventing traditional visual and spatial culture.[1]

Yung Ho Chang (Atelier FCJZ),
Hotel in Humen,
Dongguan city,
Guangdong province,
1995

In this conceptual hotel design, Yung Ho Chang adapted 16 Chinese characters, selected from the *Kangxi Dictionary* published in 1716, through four progressive steps of transcription: the introduction of poetics, walls (represented as shadows), greenery (depicted as a collage of landscape paintings) and interior space. This image was used to illustrate step 3.

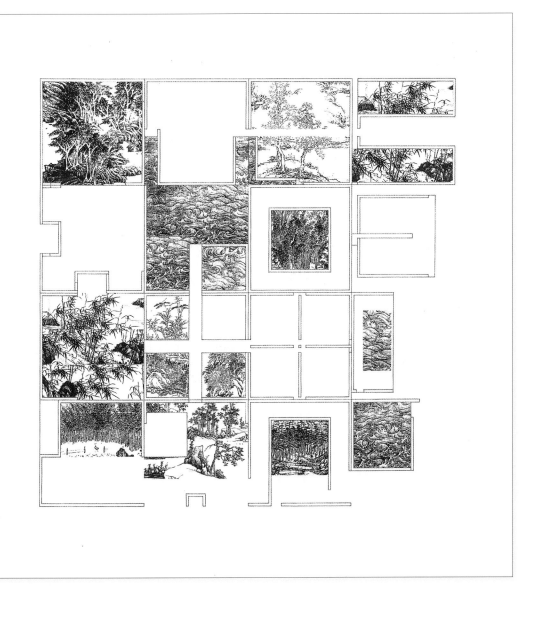

It was through their close engagement with journal editors that these visionary individuals would soon come together as a group. On 18 May 1996, Mingxian Wang, associate editor of *The Architect*, and Xiaojun Rao, a Shenzhen-based editor, co-convened the ground-breaking seminar 'Experiment and Dialogue' in Guangzhou that for the first time brought together young architects – among them Yung Ho Chang, Hua Tang, Wang Shu and Qingyun Ma – under the slogan of 'experimental architecture'. In the following few years, Wang and Rao continued to write articles to promote the idea, and a series of innovative projects were completed that demonstrated their hypothetical claims. Based on these canonical projects, such as Jiakun Liu's He Duoling Studio (Chengdu, 1997), Yung Ho Chang's Morningside Mathematics Building (Beijing, 1998) and Wang Shu's Wenzheng College Library (Suzhou University, 1999), Mingxian Wang curated the first public exhibition of Chinese experimental architects during the 20th International Union of Architects (UIA) Congress in Beijing in 1999. This landmark show triggered a huge surge of interest leading to further exhibitions and publications such as a special issue of *Time+Architecture* in 2002[2] and the influential Basis Library book series (2002) that included Yung Ho Chang's *For a Basic Architecture*, Jiakun Liu's *Now and Here*, Wang Shu's *The Beginning of Design*, Hua Tang's *Building Utopia* and Kai Cui's *Projects Report*, all calling for a focus on actual practice and operational methods.

Jiakun Liu,
Luyeyuan Stone Sculpture Museum,
Chengdu,
Sichuan province,
2002

Jiakun Liu completed his utopian novel *Project Moon* and started his practice in 1996. As a novelist and architect, his first designs were artists' studios and houses. The sculpture museum was the beginning of a series of projects in which expressions of the local and the poetic dramatically knit together.

For the experimental architects, this was a clear shift from their previously liberal attitude and alignment with literature and art to a pragmatic concern with the 'basics of architecture'. In the preface to *Feichang Architecture*, Yung Ho Chang wrote that, after returning to China for good in 1996, his practice focused more on the relationship between concept and construction and began experimenting with materials and tectonics. This was a prelude to a series of manifestos published in professional journals that included 'A Basic Architecture' (1998)[3] and 'Learning from Industrial Architecture' (2000), in which he declared his search for 'a design practice stemmed from construction rather than theory (or philosophy)'.[4] He was not alone in such a turn. Jiakun Liu began practising as an independent architect in 1996, but in contrast to Yung Ho Chang's intellectualism his approach was more realistic and robust, using local materials and construction techniques to respond to local culture and daily life. In his article 'Narrative Discourse and Low-Tech Strategy' (1997),[5] for example, he proposed integrating the literary rustic and the practical low-tech. Wang Shu, at the time described as a Dadaist architect, has recently recalled that during the 1990s he formulated 'four basic thoughts': a return to the spirit of materials, building and craftsmanship; maintaining a critical connection with social reality; expressing the existence of people within this harsh social reality; and adopting the methods used in the design of traditional Chinese gardens.[6] Although all three architects called for this same reorientation of architectural thinking, their different understandings of the basics were far from straightforward; and while all denounced 'theory' as segregated from reality, they were themselves prolific authors, actively using writing to disseminate their attitudes and thoughts.

URBANUS,
Diwang Urban Park I, Shenzhen,
Guangdong province,
2000

URBANUS's first built project. Through a series of 'urban garden' projects, the practice has established a distinctive approach focusing on observation of specific conditions and phenomena of contemporary Chinese cities, and on design as a positive intervention in urban life. This approach is still its ethos today.

Reconfiguring the System (2000–12)

Since the turn of the century, a new generation of independent architectural firms have come to the fore, many of whom have studied abroad and thus practise in ways different to those of their precursors. These include URBANUS (see pp 58–65 of this issue), Atelier Zhang Lei (later renamed AZL Architects), Atelier Deshaus (pp 88–93), Standard Architecture, Atelier Z+, Atelier Li Xinggang (pp 16–23), OPEN Architecture (pp 137–9), Vector Architects and Trace Architecture Office (TAO) (pp 39 and 132). URBANUS, for example, was founded by four partners born in the 1960s and educated in the US, and began with a series of 'urban garden' projects that integrate architecture and landscape design to respond to Shenzhen's growing demand for public space.

In contrast to their experimental predecessors of the 1990s, who carried out individual critical investigations, these independent Chinese architects are much more closely engaged with professional and social media (for example, the ABBS architectural forum, social networking website douban.com, and messaging and social media app WeChat) and their work characterised by a distinctive personal design style. Borrowing the idea from the successful Commune by the Great Wall project (Beijing, 2000), a private collection of contemporary architecture pieces designed by 12 Asian architects (and exhibited at the 2002 Venice Architecture Biennale where it received a special prize), group exhibitions and group design became new forms of dialogue among China's independent architects, resulting in projects such as the Songshan Lake scientific industrial park (Dongguan, 2002) convened by architect Kai Cui and urban planner Rongyuan Zhu, then Arata Isozaki's and Jiakun Liu's Foshou Lake art museum, hotel and residential villa complex (Nanjing, 2003); and the Jianchuan Museum Cluster (Anren, Chengdu, Sichuan province, 2004) by Yung Ho Chang and Jiakun

Liu. The work of these Chinese architects also started to appear in group exhibitions in the West, first at the Aedes Architekturforum in Berlin (2001), then at the Centre Pompidou, Paris (2003) and the Netherlands Architecture Institute (NAI) in Rotterdam (2006), all of which served to further promote and support young firms such as Atelier Deshaus and Atelier Li Xinggang, as well as the ideas of Nanda Jianzhu, a self-proclaimed group of scholar-architects at Nanjing University who had previously established the school's Graduate Institute of Architecture and included Lei Zhang and Jingxiang Zhu (see pp 40–45 of this issue).

Underpinned by the astonishing growth of Chinese universities since 1999 and the rapid increase in the numbers of accredited architectural schools (from 16 in 1998 to 60 in 2016), the rise of 'academic architects' reflected a sea-change in architectural experimentation. Former experimental architects relished this opportunity to develop their visionary understandings of the basics of architecture into a full curriculum. Yung Ho Chang founded the Graduate Centre of Architecture at Peking University, Beijing, in 2000, outlining two major research fields: construction (including basic, material, micro- and pure architecture) and urbanism (macro- and social architecture). Five years later he left Beijing and became the head of the Department of Architecture at the Massachusetts Institute of Technology (MIT). Wang Shu founded the Department of Architecture at the China Academy of Art in 2003 and devised a comprehensive syllabus for teaching Chinese experimental architecture.

The experimental architect idea, with its implications of individual attitude and peripheral resistance, was thus replaced by that of academic architect, and the critical reflections that characterised the former gave way to the systematic explorations of the latter. The Nanda Jianzhu group, several of whom had studied or taught at ETH Zurich and were determined to change Chinese architectural education, attended important gatherings and exhibitions and was soon recognised as a major force in the architectural reformation of the time. They advanced their objectives through studio teaching as much as practice within a tripartite programme including basic-, concept- and tectonic design, and conducting systematic experiments on the issues of architectonics and urbanism. These issues, targeted at practical architectural and urban situations, in turn required more rational and rigorous forms of inquiry and a revived interest in theory.

The group also launched the first bilingual architectural journal in China, the *A+D*, in which architect-turned-theorist Junyang Wang (also a Nanda Jianzhu member) published his review of Kenneth Frampton's *Studies in Tectonic Culture* (1995).[7] Later, in May 2004, the group held a seminal conference on 'Structure, Fabric, and Topography' at Nanjing University, convened by Frampton.[8] The joint endeavour of bilingual journal and academic events widely disseminated the theory of architectonics, which provided an overarching framework that circumscribed the attitudes and practices of the leading academic architects and underpinned wider reformation in design teaching. The term 'architectonic' soon became the buzzword of the 2000s. In contrast to the general suspicion of theory that dominated the previous decade, theory now became a principle that integrated and systemised disciplinary knowledge into an ontology favoured by university-based education.

The experimental architect idea, with its implications of individual attitude and peripheral resistance, was thus replaced by that of academic architect, and the critical reflections that characterised the former gave way to the systematic explorations of the latter.

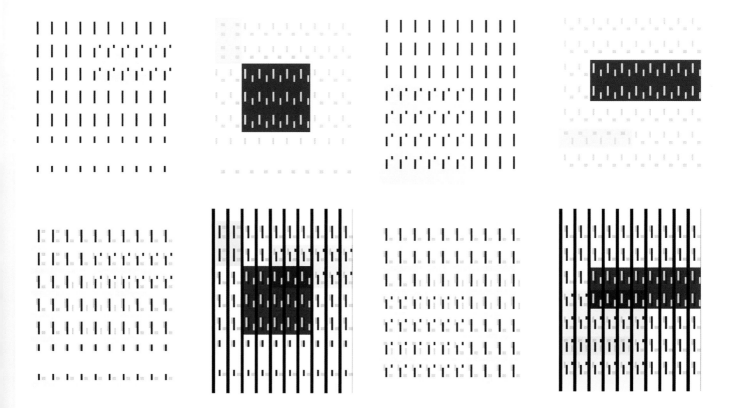

Lei Zhang,
Illustration of the Design Basics postgraduate design studio,
Graduate Institute of Architecture, Nanjing University,
2001

Lei Zhang, a key member of the Nanda Jianzhu circle and an award-winning architect himself, started the influential Design Basics research studio in 2001 and still runs it today. It focuses on spatial structure as well as the systematic recognition and abstraction of architectural elements.

An Emerging New Culture (2012–)

In many ways, 2012 was crucial for Chinese architecture. On the one hand, concerns about the country reaching the Lewisian turning point (where labour supply shifts from a surplus to a shortage) combined with political and economic crises had radically altered the perception of China as among the world's most stable economic engines. Soon after, its urban ideology shifted from development towards regeneration, and in 2014 it officially called for an end to 'oversized, xenocentric, weird' buildings.[9] On the other hand, in May 2012 Wang Shu became the first Chinese laureate of the Pritzker Prize, and a generation of architects in their 30s and 40s began to grow increasingly confident in exploring original responses to often bewildering urban and rural conditions and critical social and environmental challenges.

Another paradigm shift in design culture is thus now taking place in which the new generation of architects go beyond characteristic personal style and focus instead on innovative approaches that connect methods of investigation and the conditions of practice. Examples of this were shown in a series of 'X-Agenda' micro exhibitions at Columbia University's Studio-X in Beijing from 2012 to 2014: 'OPEN State' (OPEN Architecture), 'Intervening' (Vector Architects), 'In-situ' (TAO), 'Wind & Light' (Duoxiang Studio), 'Integrated Geometry and Poetic Scenery' (Atelier Li Xinggang – see pp 16–23), 'On the Immediacy of Objecthood and Situatedness in Architecture' (Atelier Deshaus – pp 88–93), and 'A Little Big World: Redefining Prefab for Rural and Nature' (Jingxiang Zhu – pp 40–45), all underlying a new agenda and rationale that integrates separate projects into one mega-project of long-term investigation.

Continuing the interest in the ontology of architecture since 2000, these architects are concentrating more on the capacity of investigation and process of design than on personal attitudes or outcomes. 'Research' has become a new catchword for design, and the emerging culture of design research is often sustained by close engagement with research-oriented studio teaching. In 2012, Tongji University launched a special programme that has been actively involving independent architects in Shanghai, including Bin Zhang (Atelier Z+), Shen Zhuang (Atelier Archmixing – see pp 52–7) and Yichun Liu (Atelier Deshaus). In 2014, Tsinghua University established its open-ended group design research-oriented studios inviting independent architects in Beijing to experiment with and disseminate their own agendas; they included Xinggang Li (Atelier Li Xinggang), Gong Dong (Vector Architects) and Hui Wang (URBANUS).

Vector Architects,
Seashore Library, Qinhuangdao,
Hebei province,
2015

Vector Architects founder Gong Dong completed his MArch thesis at the Illinois School of Architecture in 2001 under the instruction of Henry Plummer, a renowned advocate of the architecture of light. He has since defined architecture as an act of intervention into the natural processes of energy/spirit of a site.

Zhaoqi Ge,
Cocoons,
Space of Light third-year
design studio,
School of Architecture,
Tsinghua University,
Beijing,
2014

As a group design studio tutor at Tsinghua,
Vector Architects' founder Gong Dong
experimented with the 'space of light'.
In this student's work, interventions of
light barrels were carefully configured
to enhance an accurate and immersive
experience of time in space.

Fuelled by the rapid increase in research funding in the last 10 years, China's reformed universities have provided the interdisciplinary knowledge base, technological laboratories and new forms of collaboration needed to extend architects' capacity to respond to sophisticated conditions and specific problems, and to investigate them in more systematic and accumulative ways. Among the authors featured in this issue of 𝔇, for example, Philip F Yuan's practice Archi-Union (pp 94–101) is solidly bound to the Digital Design Research Center at Tongji University that he directs; Yichun Liu (Atelier Deshaus – pp 88–93) co-founded the cross-disciplinary practice AND-Office with structural engineer Zhun Zhang and researcher Dr Yimin Guo; Yehao Song directs the Institute for Architecture and Technology at Tsinghua University, a world-leading research base in sustainable architecture, as well as running his university-based practice SUP Atelier (pp 74–9); Xin Zhang, a renowned scholar in lighting design, collaborates with practices such as DnA Design and Architecture and He Wei Studio to explore the design potential of lighting-led architecture (pp 102–9); and our own LanD Studio for Design Research is a think-tank that develops prototypical projects to create new working models of design research.

Over the past quarter century, experimental architecture in China has undergone several paradigm shifts, from individual resistance and personal reflection to a return to basics, principles and systems, and to connecting contemporary design with research into advanced technologies and the humanities. Four threads of thought have characterised the evolution of its design culture: the main yet contradictory themes of 'creation' and 'experimentation' in the 1990s being completed superseded from 2004 by 'ontology' and 'research', the former centred on principle and theory, the latter on investigation and agenda. In the ongoing move towards approach, process and modus operandi, the latest generation of architects are practising with innovative forms of investigation and collaboration that allow them to respond to a rapidly changing environment in a more specific and sensitive way. 𝔇

Notes
1. Yung Ho Chang, *Feichang Architecture*, Heilongjiang Science and Technology Press (Harbin), 1997.
2. *Chinese Experimental Architecture: Time + Architecture*, 5, 2002.
3. Yung Ho Chang, 'A Basic Architecture', *The Architect*, 84 (10), 1998, pp 27–37.
4. Yung Ho Chang and Lufeng Zhang, 'Learning from Industrial Architecture', *World Architecture*, 7, 2000, pp 22–3.
5. Jiakun Liu, 'Narrative Discourse and Low-Tech Strategy', *The Architect*, 78 (10), 1997, pp 46–50.
6. Wang Shu, 'Miscellaneous Notes on Architectural Education', *Architectural Journal*, 12, 2017, pp 1–8.
7. Qun Wang (later renamed Junyang Wang), 'Reading Frampton's *Studies in Tectonic Culture*', *A+D*, 1, 2001, pp 69–80 (part 1) and *A+D*, 2, 2001, pp 69–80 (part 2).
8. Kenneth Frampton, *Studies in Tectonic Culture*, MIT Press (Cambridge, MA), 1995.
9. As referred to by President Xi Jingping at the Colloquium on Cultural Work at the Great Hall of the People, Beijing, on 15 October 2014.

Atelier Deshaus,
Golden Ridge Upper-Cloister,
Chengde,
Hebei province,
due for completion 2019

In recent years Atelier Deshaus founder Yichun Liu has collaborated closely with structural engineers to experiment with a redefined use of structure as a medium of association with our bodies and of adaptation to a site's features. As such, structure is no longer the material evidence of forces, but becomes part of the culture.

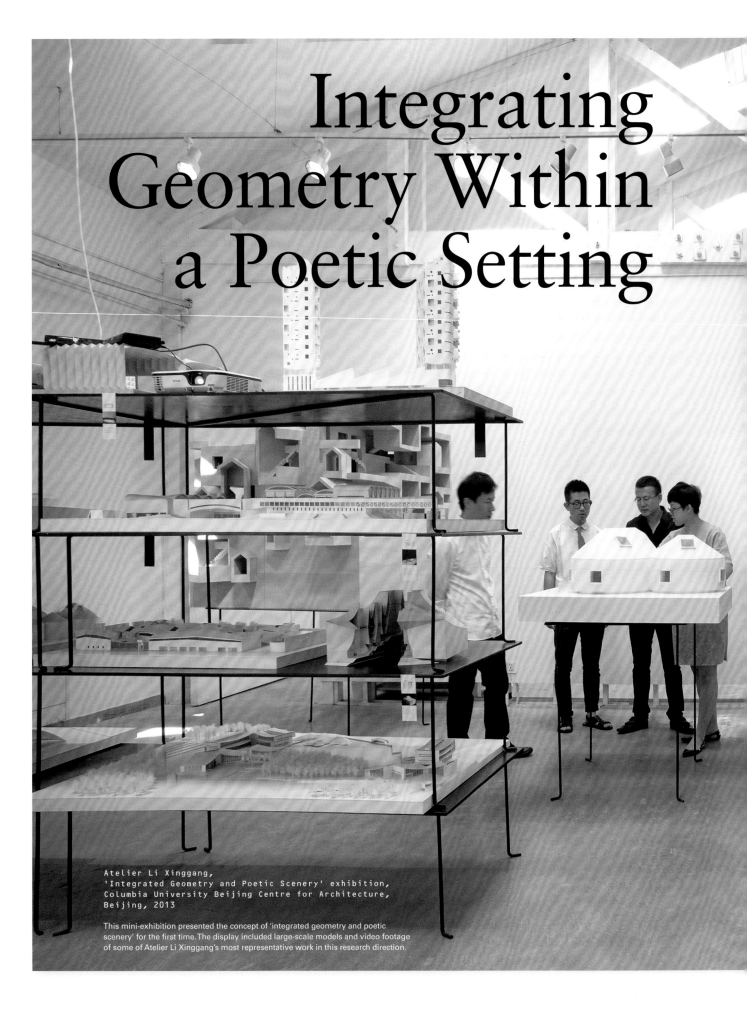

Integrating Geometry Within a Poetic Setting

Atelier Li Xinggang,
'Integrated Geometry and Poetic Scenery' exhibition,
Columbia University Beijing Centre for Architecture,
Beijing, 2013

This mini-exhibition presented the concept of 'integrated geometry and poetic
scenery' for the first time. The display included large-scale models and video footage
of some of Atelier Li Xinggang's most representative work in this research direction.

Xinggang Li

Steering a Path Between the Artificial and the Natural

Anodyne, internationally identical urban environments are leaving the human spirit bereft. According to **Xinggang Li** – a practising architect and visiting professor at Tianjin University – what is needed is an injection of poetics and a heightened awareness of context. Here he sets out the vision on which his award-winning architectural office Atelier Li Xinggang bases its work, and highlights some of its recent projects where an interrelationship between the artificial and the natural makes for inspiring and harmonious settings in which to live, learn or play.

The following reflection, research and practice originated from broad interests in Chinese cities, architecture, gardens and settlements. Proceeding from these subjects, and gradually focusing on the philosophy of humankind and the universe, the poetic tradition, the practice of the ideal, as well as their relationship with contemporary Chinese reality, it is possible to base practice on the idea of 'integrated geometry and poetic scenery' and correct and broaden the traditional boundaries of architecture. The inclusion and further emphasis of nature as an ontological element parallel to space, structure, form and construction in architecture may lead to a new type of contemporary architecture that embraces the future, and help to achieve a poetic creation of living space.

Lost Tradition and Grave, Diverse Reality

Artificiality is inseparable from and crucially significant to life, nature and the spiritual world. To the human eye, an environment that is created with an appropriate level of artificial intervention into nature is more 'beautiful' than pure nature itself. This is, in fact, ingrained in the human spirit. The intervention of artificiality within nature takes different forms in different cultural contexts. Royal burial grounds serve as a good example of this. The Egyptian pyramids are gigantic, highly precise geometric volumes that stand alone, entirely separated from nature, representing the greatness and independence of humankind. This can be considered as 'self-completed artificiality'. However, a number of China's Eastern Qing imperial tombs represent a distinctly different composition, based on the principles of feng shui. Contrary to the design of Egyptian pyramids, the natural formation of the hills guards, surrounds and pays obeisance to the burial grounds. The artificial order and the natural elements complement each other in coexistence. This can be considered as 'complementary artificiality and nature'. This mutually complementary state of being, between the natural and the man-made, is the ideal approach to the creation of space for human activities. It must be emphasised that such a state of poetic scenery is not unique to Chinese or oriental societies, but transcends culture, geographical location and time; it is a universal perception and creation shared by all civilisations.

However, this precious and rational tradition is disappearing. In the contemporary world, especially in contemporary China, there are conflicts between ecological resources and development, as well as between land resources and population growth. Furthermore, we are confronted with the challenges brought about by the inappropriate strategies used to deal with these conflicts: namely, overtly artificial living environments that gradually push people away from the long-standing ideals of life and the mutual affinity between humankind and nature. Hundreds of cities have acquired the same appearance, and the urban environment is no longer a dynamic and multifaceted place where human life and nature are mutually dependent and coexist. At its root, this is the result of the problematic relationship between the artificial and the natural in urban life and in architecture-related fields. This 'grave reality' presents a relationship that is not only

imbalanced, instead of appropriate, but also fragmented, instead of interactive. As a subject that specifically deals with living space, and a profession that creates it, how does architecture play a vital role in constructing and correcting reality and achieving the ideal urban environment?

A Corrective Architectural Theory

Atelier Li Xinggang's practice covers a broad range of subjects such as geography, technology and social, economic and cultural conditions. It can be considered a 'multiple reality'. One of the office's key aims has been to locate a design principle and strategy that is rooted in site specification and local conditions, and whose form also transcends time and place. With a view to this, it has sought to establish a stable set of tools, means and languages that not only express notions specific to the time and place, but also focus on a much broader concern of the ideal living conditions for humankind.

'Integrated Geometry and Poetic Scenery' was an exhibition organised by Atelier Li Xinggang at the Columbia University Beijing Centre for Architecture in 2013. Its title summarises a new architectural and spatial paradigm that includes 'nature' into the fundamental elements of architectural identity. It points towards both an ideal that is based on universal human nature, and the possibility of correcting contemporary architectural theory.

'Poetic Scenery' refers to a spatial experience that is fundamentally natural and spiritual. 'Integrated Geometry' refers to the function of the architectural body. Based on the principle of geometry, important elements such as structure, space, form and construction interact and evolve to provide the space with a concise order and distinct spatial arrangement, routes and interface, in order to obtain an antithesis to nature, while at the same time embracing, resembling, appropriating and even 'creating' nature. This exercise, which grants the user an experience of 'poetic scenery', is artificial and material. 'Integrated geometry and poetic scenery' is thus an approach to practice that drives architectural elements based on geometrical principles such as structure, space, form and construction to interact with each other and evolve, and therefore creates a spatial poetics closely related to and participating in nature. The whole that is created by the complementary relationship between artificiality and nature becomes the ideal living space for the user.

Strategies for Ideal Practice

Jixi Museum, completed by Atelier Li Xinggang in 2013, is located in the centre of the historic city of Jixi. On the eastern peak of Mount Huang in Anhui province, surrounded by mountains and waterways, it houses displays on themes of local history and culture. The form of the roof imitates the mountains, its rhythmic rise and fall and its texture blending in with the city's surroundings so that it becomes part of the natural environment of Jixi. Trees on the site were retained in the landscaping. Several gardens, courtyards and alleyways are arranged around the plantation. Combined with the water channels that converge at the main courtyard, they create an urban sitting room for the town. Triangular roof truss units not only generate the roof's continuous form, but also present a winding internal space that stretches to the distance through perspective. Outside, a 24-hour ascending promenade route leads visitors to the viewing platform on the roof at the southeast part of the building, overlooking the roof, the courtyard and, beyond, the mountains. The manmade structure, the historical town and the natural plantation communicate with each other and with the distant landscape, bringing a poetic spatial experience into visitors' minds. It is just as the poet Runyang Lu (1841–1915) described in his couplet: 'Living in the shadow of the tree, I go with the flow; mountains are in view as soon as I open the door, so I do not need to go far for my consciousness of nature.'[1]

The museum's design harmonises with its setting in various ways. The continuous roof's rhythmic rise and fall echoes the surrounding hills and waterways of the old city of Jixi. The courtyards are landscaped around pre-existing trees, and combine with internal alleyways and streams gathered at the main courtyard to create an urban sitting room.

Seen from the viewing platform on top of the southeast end of the building, the undulating roof forms interspersed with trees, against the backdrop of distant hills, offer a poetic experience to visitors.

Atelier Li Xinggang,
Jixi Museum,
Anhui province,
2013

The open working model of the museum shows how the varying sizes of triangular roof truss structural units are positioned in sequence to create a dynamic roof form and a winding internal space.

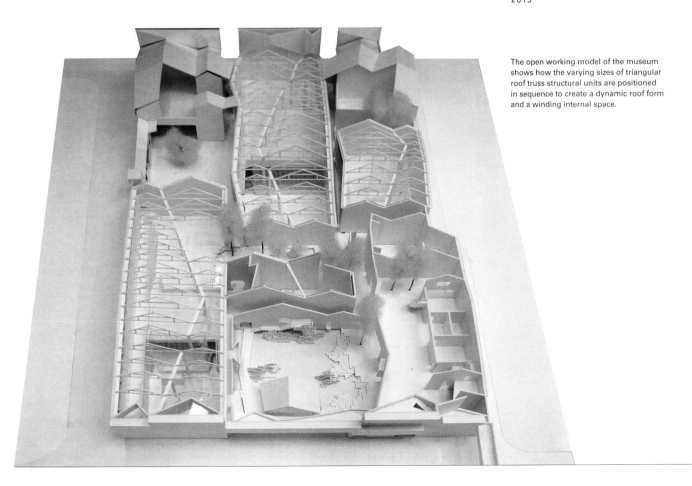

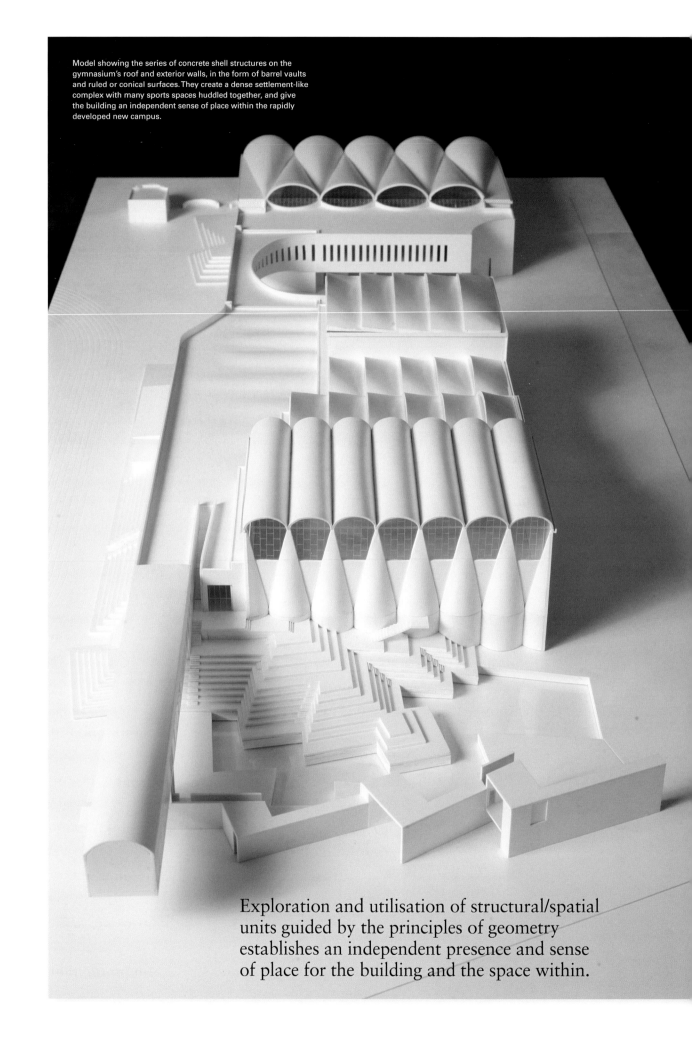

Model showing the series of concrete shell structures on the
gymnasium's roof and exterior walls, in the form of barrel vaults
and ruled or conical surfaces. They create a dense settlement-like
complex with many sports spaces huddled together, and give
the building an independent sense of place within the rapidly
developed new campus.

Exploration and utilisation of structural/spatial
units guided by the principles of geometry
establishes an independent presence and sense
of place for the building and the space within.

Students playing sports under the Y-shaped columns in the sports hall for ball games. Different scales and forms in structural elements respond to different stages of body movement, forming a strong sense of space that calls for a poetic emotional experience.

The gymnasium of the new campus in Tianjin University, an Atelier Li Xinggang project completed in 2015, is situated in the new education park, around the middle section of Haihe River, Tianjin. It is a multifunctional sports complex that serves for indoor training, as well as teaching and research purposes. The design arranges spaces for various types of sports along a linear public area, according to their specific requirements and functions. A series of concrete shell structures in the form of barrel vaults, flat surfaces and conical surfaces, either in single units or combined, are applied to the roof and exterior walls. This design strategy provides a suitable span for the sports spaces, as well as clerestory lighting and thermal ventilation. A reserved yet dynamically formed architectural outline creates a dense settlement-like complex with many sports spaces nested together. Exploration and utilisation of structural/spatial units guided by the principles of geometry establishes an independent presence and sense of place for the building and the space within. It creates a spontaneous dialogue with the site, which is situated in a new campus that is fragmented and incoherent due to its rapid development. Meanwhile, the different scales and forms in the spatial structure respond to the different stages of body movement in sports, as if interacting with and complementing these dynamic and natural human sceneries, forming a strong sense of space that calls for a poetic emotional experience.

Atelier Li Xinggang,
Gymnasium of New Campus,
Tianjin University,
Tianjin,
2015

Natural clerestory lighting in the swimming pool illuminates the structure and reflects the fluctuation of the waves and the moving bodies.

Atelier Li Xinggang,
'Miniature Beijing'
– conversion of
No 28 Dayuan Hutong,
Beijing,
2017

Axonometric of this typical multiple-occupancy courtyard house in the old city of Beijing, converted into an orderly community. The complex, composed of several linear concrete structural/spatial units, includes five courtyard apartments and a public garden, connected by a semi-open primary alleyway and smaller alleys leading from the lane outside.

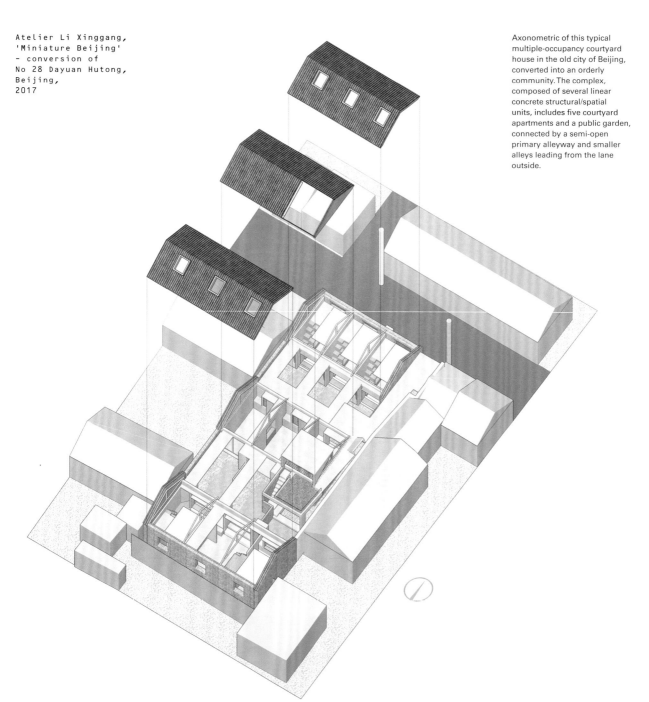

Several linear concrete structural/spatial units form the elementary spaces within the complex. Each contains a courtyard that is varied in size and shape.

The five apartments converted within the existing courtyard house form a miniature urban neighbourhood, containing gardens of different sizes and shapes. All of the apartments have a spacious and well-lit main living room, benefiting from a view of the garden.

In 2017 Atelier Li Xinggang completed the conversion of No 28 Dayuan Hutong, titled 'Miniature Beijing'. Located in the old city area of Beijing that is dominated by hutongs (narrow streets), the traditional courtyard house of 262 square metres (2,820 square feet) is transformed into five apartments with self-contained courtyards, as well as a public space that hosts a café and a teahouse. Turning from the noisy urban commercial streets into the peaceful and leisurely hutong district, then through the main hutongs outside to a semi-external alleyway and a further smaller lane, separate paths lead to the north and south courtyard apartments of different sizes and configurations. Several linear concrete structural/spatial units form the elementary spaces within the complex. Each contains a courtyard that is varied in size and shape. The main living room of each apartment is spacious and bright, benefiting from a view of the garden. Travelling further south along the main alleyway, passing the café and teahouse, visitors reach the small public garden at the rear and arrive at the platform of the pavilion elevated above the courtyard via a set of concrete steps on the side. With the setting sun as the background, the profound scenery – composed of the stacked roofs in the old city area, the ancient trees, flying pigeons and the new city high-rises in the distance – induces a state of contemplation in visitors.

A flight of concrete steps leads up to the platform of the pavilion elevated above the courtyard. Here, visitors and residents can immerse themselves in contemplating the profoundly poetic scenery composed of stacked roofs in the old city, ancient trees, flying pigeons and the new city high-rises in the distance, against the setting sun.

This small experimental project investigates the possibility of the densification of Beijing's urban structures, and the viable transformation of a courtyard to a neighbourhood, similar to the molecular subdivision of cells. It investigates the possibility of the return of Beijing's infamously crowded courtyard houses occupied by many households to small collective courtyard dwellings. Here, the ideal living environment can be achieved: house and garden can unite harmoniously, and the poetic quality of space occupied by the individual's daily routine can exist in parallel with the poetic quality of a sacred public space in a new multifunctional urban zone.

A Paradigm for Creating Space

These three Atelier Li Xinggang projects present not only the multiple realities that confront architects in practice, but also multiple experiments and their results in various environments where the artificial and the natural maintain different relationships. They lead to the conclusion that there are five strategies which may generally be applied: introducing architecture as part of the landscape to the site; combining structural and spatial qualities in units; artificiality and nature interacting with and mutually transforming each other; clearly conveying the defined context and atmosphere of the spatial field through structure; and narrative guiding the poetic scenery.

These general strategies build an organic whole to present a paradigm for the creation of space. Through the arrangement of space and the management of positions, the combination and layering of structural and spatial units, together with a dramatic narrative that guides the user to reach a crescendo in spatial experience, an ideal living space is achieved that uses artificial and materialistic 'integrated geometry' (the architectural body) as a tool to create a natural and spiritual 'poetic scenery' (the spatial poetry).

This paradigm could be called 'immersion in the scenery'. A body that is immersed in the spatial experience is emotionally unified with it; the process of immersing oneself is one of approaching until one arrives at and finally assumes a vantage point. The 'scenery' is the spatial experience that the surroundings create. It emphasises the journey of bodily experience of time and space, and the exact moment and state when one arrives at the location and obtains the specific spatial experience and is immersed in the scenery. Atelier Li Xinggang does not intend architecture and space only to become a visual representation that can be viewed, but focuses on the interaction between manmade structures and their natural scenery – and, as a result, offers people a poetic existence and lifestyle. ⌂

Note
1. Runyang Lu was the highest score achiever in the Imperial Exam in the 13th year of the Tongzhi reign, Qing dynasty. The Chinese philosopher Shi Hu (1891–1962) later handwrote the couplets in calligraphy while living in Jixi, and they are now in the collection of Jixi Museum.

Xin Wang and Qiuye Jin

Arc

A Contemporary Chinese

Linyue Wei,
'Stream Bank Blocked with Boats',
'Shanshui Perspective'
teaching experiment,
School of Architectural Art,
China Academy of Art,
Xiangshan, China, 2015

This work by second-year student Wei Linyue embodies the traditional Chinese concept of 'instant poetry'. It evokes occasions in the past when a canal was jammed with ships, and it could take months to sort out the congestion. Chaotic as the situation seemed, life on the boats still went on and the boats stuck in the canal temporarily formed a street.

adia

Garden Experiment

Modernity need not be synonymous with abstraction or with a lack of cultural resonance. The art of China's historical literate elite, and the environments they surrounded themselves with, are ripe with inspiration for a formal language that is relevant today. The academic group Arcadia and the related design practice Zaoyuan Gardening Studio have been investigating how aspects of these artificial landscapes might spur a new poetics in Chinese architecture. Two of Arcadia's founders, **Xin Wang and Qiuye Jin**, describe their work – spanning teaching, research and built projects.

Named after the mythical lost garden, Arcadia is an academic group dedicated to contemporary experimentation in Chinese gardens, as well as a platform for open discussion in related fields. Its work includes teaching, architectural design, theoretical research, publishing, exhibitions and other academic activities. Its eponymous journal *Arcadia* collects research results on Chinese gardens published by China's forward-looking theoreticians and designers.

Contemporary experimentation in Chinese gardens is an important supplement to contemporary architectural practice in China. Its values are guided by the country's traditional natural philosophy, and its aesthetic attitude and formal basis are to be found in the elegant lifestyle of the elite Chinese scholar-artists known as the 'literati'. It proposes a new direction for architecture: that of following nature's laws.

Arcadia's teaching is rooted in the elementary design courses of the School of Architectural Art at the China Academy of Art in Hangzhou. It is a teaching innovation experiment that takes the academic direction of 'Reconstructing a Chinese Native Architecture', as proposed by Professor Wang Shu. The Arcadia group set up the Zaoyuan Gardening Studio, which is devoted to the transformation of the achievements of teaching and research into architectural practice in China, including the design of buildings, gardens and exhibition spaces.

Arcadia,
volumes 1 and 2,
2015 and 2017

Volume 1, *Painting and Garden* (2015) and Volume 2, *Illusion and Reality* (2017), of Arcadia's journal both discussed the transformation of traditional poetry and aesthetics into contemporary architectural practice, including the topics of traditional painting, gardens, space perspective and limited construction.

Teaching Experiments

'Shanshui Perspective' was a teaching experiment that served as the second-year course for the School of Architectural Art from 2010 to 2016. It derived from the optical characteristics and compositional norms of *shanshui* – the traditional Chinese art of landscape painting using brush and ink. Xin Wang explored the unique mode of spatial cognition and poetic circumstance modelling in *shanshui* from an innovative perspective, and made it serve for architectural education through the transformation of a series of formal languages used in various old paintings. In Chinese natural philosophy and aesthetics, nature is presented in architecture by the narrative. All naturalised gestures will become the new starting point and appraisal standard for architecture. In order to make a natural architecture, we need to conceive in a natural way, just like our ancient painters. In 2013, Qiuye Jin curated an exhibition under the same title, and in 2015 Wang published his book *An Architecture Towards Shanshui*.

Siqi Xing, 'Wooden Hall in Dongtian', 'Shanshui Perspective' teaching experiment, School of Architectural Art,
China Academy of Art,
Xiangshan,
China,
2015

Dongtian, a concept in Taoism, literally means the world inside a cave. Whatever its size, a *dongtian* is a complete microworld not inferior to the macroworld. Second-year student Siqi Xing's project creates a *dongtian* in which the building represents nature and imitates a cage, while the space within (an elegant interior) is hidden underneath.

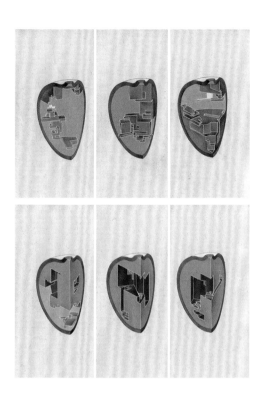

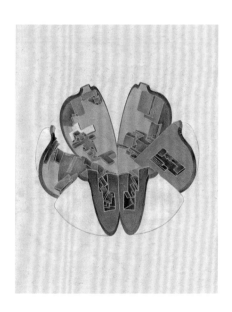

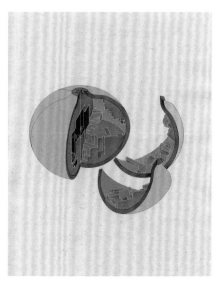

'Artefacts Space' was another second-year course at the School, from 2013 to 2016. The artefacts of the Chinese literati used to be part of their aesthetics of daily life, and reflected their intellectual world and thoughts on design. They were the spiritual equivalents of the unity of architecture, gardening and painting. In the manner of the well-known line from William Blake's poem *Auguries of Innocence* – 'To see a world in a grain of sand' – literati artefacts embody the real world while projecting it; they are an 'agent' for a cultural stratum to understand, imagine and construct their real world. Moreover, these artefacts of ingenuity and feelings had practical everyday uses. The first assignment for the students was to design a bowl, a tea-container, a birdcage, a long-handled spoon or suchlike. In this process, the students' interest in everyday life was activated prior to their understanding of architectural design. 'Artefacts Space' helped them to reflect on daily life and to revive the traditional humanistic spirit. Thus, the long-forgotten artefacts of the literati were revived to be handy gardens, as well as a poetic form of architecture.

Jiafeng Li,
'Six Segmental Worlds in a Melon',
'Artefacts Space' teaching experiment,
School of Architectural Art,
China Academy of Art,
Xiangshan,
China,
2015

Second-year student Jiafeng Li's project creates six poetic worlds in a melon. It is not only an 'architectural toy' for architects but also an artefact for literati to play with.

These artefacts of ingenuity and feelings had practical everyday uses.

One of the most celebrated and extraordinary works in the history of Chinese painting, *The Night Revels of Han Xizai* – originally painted in the 10th century by Hongzhong Gu but known today through a 12th-century copy – also provides a great insight into the Chinese garden. It was the inspiration for the 2017 graduation project of one of Xin Wang's students, Yu Sun, titled 'Highlights from the Opera'. The project's aim was to analyse the hidden 'space-time structure' of the painting through careful observation of the characters' actions and the articles' positions, and then to design a stage with similar 'geometric tricks' made clear by the type of architecture and architectural graphic induction. The result is a magical translation of the ambiguous 'dreaming' aspects of the painting into clear architectural narratives. It features a cross motif that originates from the marginal spaces in Chinese gardens, and also from the expression of traditional Chinese 'highlights from the opera'. This idea, derived from study of the architectural diagram by scholars such as John Hejduk and Yonghe Zhang, is also a response to Wang Shu. By proposing the 'garden as a method', he intended to warn Chinese architects against falling into a vain exploration of styles when talking about 'tradition'.

Yu Sun,
'Highlights from the Opera',
School of Architectural Art,
China Academy of Art,
Xiangshan,
China,
2017

The 12th-century painting *The Night Revels of Han Xizai* presents various scenes of a banquet with different placements of furniture, directions of figures, and the interlacing of virtual and actual images. Sun Yu's graduation project converts the painting into an architectural structure using a cross-shaped stage which adopts the design of Chinese gardens and indicates the significance of corners.

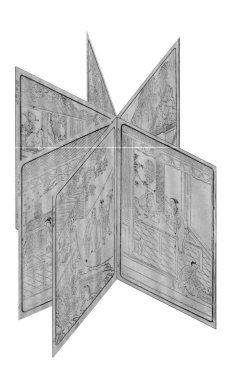

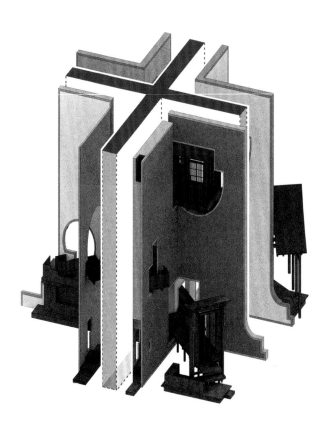

The picture is the integration of space design and opera scripts. The four corners present four acts of a play with the appearance, gestures and speeches of figures.

A Pavilion in the Silk Road Art Park

One of the Zaoyuan Gardening Studio's recent projects is the Red Pavilion in the Silk Road Art Park, Quanzhou, Fujian province, completed in 2015 .

The *dacuo* houses of Quanzhou are long stretches of red: red roofs, red walls, red ground, different materials of red interweaving to form a richly varied 'red community'. In this place of hundreds of years of 'red', Wang had been dreaming of building a red house for more than a decade. The pavilion was a renovation project commissioned by the Government of Taishang District, with a design and construction span of no more than two months. The original structure was an unfiished concrete frame.

Facing such an urgent task, Wang came up with the strategy of giving the building a wide robe with a large sleeve, recalling the garment of an ancient literati. The sweeping roof is like an enormous veil or umbrella. The red lauan-wood roof grille makes the building a continuous shelter. The gable walls are the two sleeves, and the brocade-like ground resembles waves surging underfoot. All the elements are red but constructed with different materials. The combination of bricks and stones is a local building technology that was applied to the new pavilion. The bricks and stones were salvaged from old buildings demolished by the roadside, which would otherwise have been removed as 'rubbish'.

The dacuo *houses of Quanzhou are long stretches of red: red roofs, red walls, red ground, different materials of red interweaving to form a richly varied 'red community'.*

Zaoyuan Gardening Studio,
Red Pavilion,
Silk Road Art Park,
Quanzhou,
Fujian province,
China,
2015

View of the northeast facade. The enormous umbrella-shaped roof originates from the roof ridge of the traditional *dacuo* houses of Quanzhou. Majestic as it is, the pavilion acts as a mountain, providing a restful interior. A long ramp leading to the roof, then descending into a moon-shaped hollow, is the entrance to the building.

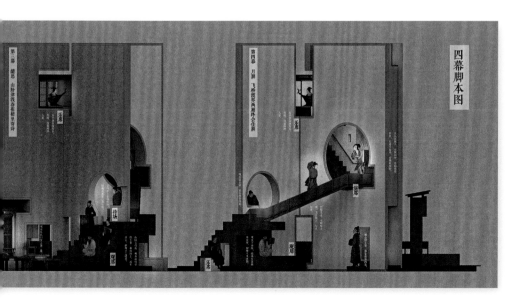

Extending indoor activities to the outdoors enables the courtyard to become the living room and the pine trees to become the roof. Furniture-like objects are furniture of nature. In this sense, Chinese gardens are roofless architecture and thus part of the residents' life.

A Modern Literati Garden in Zhejiang Province

'Tea Party under the Pine Shade' is a garden in Zhang village, Anji county, Zhejiang province, designed by the Zaoyuan Gardening Studio. The result of rural teacher Mr Fang's dream of owning a literati garden, it covers only 60 square metres (650 square feet) of land and was completed in 2016 to a very limited budget.

The garden's name refers to the way Chinese people define their space: a combination of human event ('Tea Party') and atmosphere ('Pine Shade'). In China, the pine tree represents a sense of ancient elegance. The garden comes from painting; so the sense of the painting (picturesqueness) comes before the gardening activities.

The core of the design is how to reconsider 'nature' in modern gardening. A productive but greatly disparaged way is to represent nature with the natural gestures of the architecture itself. Traditional gardens use the 'mountain house' to remind people of the mountains, thus turning the artificial environment into one full of natural meanings. A mountain-like pedestal supports the house, and water winds along beneath it. Here, the pedestal is like a continuous piece of furniture, combining the tea tables, benches, trees, springs, mountain paths and stone lanterns into a single whole. It is a compound building, a piece of embodied nature. And the house is a tribute to the Yuan dynasty painter Zan Ni's 'Rong Xi Zhai', a cabinet-like tiny hut that could only be entered by crawling into it. The mountain and the house represent two different ways to drink tea: one natural, the other formalised.

The garden can be glimpsed through two moon-like gates, bringing in new scenery to the neighbourhood. It was built collaboratively by the local villagers. Small as it is, it has brought a breath of fresh air to a dreary setting and became a big local event.

Zaoyuan Gardening Studio,
'Tea Party under the Pine Shade',
Zhang village,
Anji county,
Zhejiang province,
China,
2016

The garden's scenery is framed by two moon gates, intended to create a new perspective view. First, they frame a detached place, like a window open to a tea party in the Song Dynasty. Second, they build a poetic border between the neighbours, and people will look in from outside with care and love.

An Exploration of Literati Garden Types

A feature of the China Academy of Art's Hangzhou campus is the Museum of Folk Art. This is the site for the Zaoyuan Gardening Studio's 'Gardens as the Spatial Gesture of Chinese Literati: Five Types', created in 2017.

This design is the theme space of the 'Contemporary Suzhou Garden and Living Art Exhibition', and is the first time that a contemporary gardening context has entered the museum systematically. Five types of new gardens are provided to represent different kinds of cultural attitudes of the traditional Chinese litcrati. They serve as narrative spaces, like situational stages that can be experienced in person, becoming a voice-over for the items all around to show daily life in a Chinese garden.

The essential question of the Chinese garden is how to represent nature with architecture and how to conceptualise nature with the formal language. Wang has called it an 'imitation of *shanshui*', a highly artificialised poetic pattern language. Different components of the traditional garden – such as the door, the window, the boat, the bench, the screen, the bridge and the cave – are extracted, then recombined to form new meanings and new types. The five types are: Mountain House Overlooking the Distance; Sleeping House in a Turbulent Wave; Stepping House In and Out of a Painting; Tiny House Holding the Knees; and Distant House with a Faraway Thought.

Zaoyuan Gardening Studio,
'Gardens as the Spatial Gesture of Chinese Literati: Five Types',
Museum of Folk Art,
China Academy of Art,
Hangzhou,
China,
2017

This is the prologue of the exhibition space and embodies the first of the five types: 'Mountain House Overlooking the Distance'. It is a combination of a roof, a screen and a *guan mao* chair (a classic piece of furniture in the shape of an antique official's hat). When the screen is opened, it reveals a view of the roof, which represents the mountain.

Implications for Architecture

In the dualistic system of traditional Chinese architecture, individualised and freely laid-out gardens are in extreme contrast to the geometrically planned palaces that embody power structure and social order. The physical form and spatial characteristics of Chinese traditional gardens have varied over time. But their non-Euclidean spatial composition, their shifting perspectives and their emphasis on body perception can inspire the imagination of Chinese architects in search of an alternative architectural language other than abstraction and purism. Because of this, experiments in gardens based on the traditional cultural spirit are at the very core of the search for a native Chinese architectural language.

Thanks to the theoretical contribution of pioneers in the study of Chinese gardens, such as Dunzhen Liu (1897–1968) and Jun Tong (1900–1983), their unique spatial forms and aesthetic pursuits are widely known. A large amount of surveying and quantitative analysis has made gardens an organic part of modern architectural research. The work and teaching of architect Jizhong Feng (1915–2009) emphasised 'meaning' and 'structuring' as central to contemporary garden practice, and re-established the relationship between contemporary architectural practice and traditional literati art. In this light, Wang Shu believes that the artistic language of different historical periods should be treated differently, and the modern transformation of traditional design language should be regarded as a process of discriminating, filtering and reconstructing. His extensive output shows that gardens not only can be transformed into a source of modern spatial types through scale conversion, but also into a kind of cultural landscape – that is, the 'Shanshui Perspective', which is quite different from the abstract purity of modernism. Yugan Dong deeply explores the 'physicality' of gardens (probably the Eastern counterpart of Phenomenology), another alternative approach to 'conceptual' modern architecture.

Arcadia and the Zaoyuan Gardening Studio continue the explorations of Wang Shu and Yugan Dong, perfectly combining 'everydayness' and 'abstractness' while at the same time integrating with the in-depth study of traditional Chinese artefacts, and exploring a poetic and symbolic form of language with so-called 'accessorial buildings' – which is both typological and rich in physical characteristics, and has become a unique direction in contemporary garden design. When Wang Shu put forward the concept of 'natural construction', he was referring not only to an ecological and organic type of construction done in a natural way, but also to a poetic scheme of contemplating nature and drawing an abstract form language from it, which is quite different from the sentimental naturalistic attitude. Zaoyuan Gardening Studio's practice further abolishes the ideological factors attached to architecture, and introduces a discussion of traditional formal language into a field of pure aesthetics, a realm of illusory life scenarios unrelated to politics, the sublime but mundane spiritual space of the literati of the Ming and Qing dynasties. ◍

Lost

and

Pingping Dou

Reinventing Multi-Screen Adaptable Architecture

Li Hua / TAO (Trace Architecture Office),
Split Courtyard House,
Hutong near White Pagoda Temple,
Beijing,
2015

To accommodate today's young single citizens, the compact site is divided into four sets of rental apartments, forming a pinwheel configuration, each with a studio room and a tiny private yard.

Found

One of traditional Chinese architecture's most distinctive features is the partition of interior spaces by multiple, mostly moveable screens. These offer many benefits in terms of not only the practical aspects of spatial flexibility and climate control, but also less tangible aural, psychological and ornamental effects. Guest-Editor **Pingping Dou** explores their history and function, and illustrates their potential for use in today's search for architectural adaptability through three recent projects in Beijing.

Wen Sun,
Illustration of traditional Chinese screens,
1891

This late 19th-century illustration to the classic Chinese novel
A Dream of Red Mansions (1791) shows a series of interconnected interior spaces divided by a variety of lavishly decorated screens. The lattice screens and layers of curtains of the two alcove beds define the rooms' most private areas.

Orthodox Western architecture has long been framed as solid and static objects, and thus as a means to stabilise society and represent permanence. It emphasises the completed building as a finished project for a particular user and location. However, it overtly reduces buildings to an explicit set of specifications, and excessively subjects space to usage. Alongside the mainstream discourse, there has been a growing awareness of architecture as a dynamic equilibrium of everyday process. The notion of adaptability introduces time and the unknown causes of change to architecture. Given the instability of contemporary society and the diversity of urban lifestyles, the imperative is even more pressing today than when adaptability was first introduced, in the 1950s, as a general architectural principle of resistance and extension of functionalism.[1]

John Habraken, one of the pioneers who first identified adaptability in architecture, promoted the two-part strategy of 'support and infill' in mass housing, starting in the early 1960s.[2] His peers in Europe, and later (since 1996) the international commission CIB W104 Open Building Implementation, have developed the theory and examined and promoted residential open buildings worldwide, such as the PSSHAK (Primary Support Structures and Housing Assembly Kits) housing estate at Adelaide Road, London (1979) and the NEXT21 housing project in Osaka (1994).[3] Adaptable architecture implies a dilution of authorial and regulatory control from the very parties who execute the process; hence it always faces a dilemma in implementation. Meanwhile, ubiquitous traditional residential typologies with simple plans and sections, generous volumes and structural capacities can respond to volatile societal changes in an adaptive manner, though this might not be recognised at the time.

Architectural or Ornamental?

Differing from the variety of styles in the development of Western architecture, Chinese traditional architecture appears forever consistent. In most situations, minor interior variations are sufficient to fulfil changing needs, and therefore the overall morphology achieves a historical continuity. Take, for example, *siheyuan*: courtyards surrounded by buildings on all four sides, which constituted the basic pattern used for residences, palaces, temples and government offices throughout Chinese history. With courtyards varying in size, shape and number, *siheyuan* could adapt to the great variety of urban situations. The same typology of rectangular plan, timber beams and columns, and tiled pitched roof creates a structural space, leaving its interior open to be appropriated later. The structure and form of the house and courtyard generally does not change, whereas connections and divisions are constantly altered. The timber beam-and-column structure has similar advantages to a contemporary frame structure, providing a high level of flexibility in spatial arrangement. A range of 'screens' attached to this principal frame gradually evolved into the most distinctive artistic feature of Chinese architecture. Fixed or freestanding, made of different kinds of materials and often connected by hinges, they had both practical and ornamental uses. However, they were considered as artistic, because the convention within Chinese architecture was to focus on the structural system as the essential factor, known as *damuzuo* (major carpentry), and to regard the partitioning and furnishing, known as *xiaomuzuo* (minor carpentry), as decorative and hence non-architectural matters.[4]

Spatial and Environmental Hierarchy

The 19th-century German architect Gottfried Semper explained the origins of architecture through the lens of anthropology, and identified four basic elements: hearth, mound, roof and enclosure.[5] In recent years, scholars and architects have extended this layered categorisation – eg shell, services and scenery (Francis Duffy, 1990)[6]; site, structure, skin, services, space plan and stuff (Stewart Brand, 1994)[7]; or structure, skin, scenery, services and access (Bernard Leupen, 2006)[8] – into an effective tool in analysing and improving adaptability. From the point of view of layer framework, an exceptional characteristic of Chinese architecture is that the skin and interior ought to be better conceived in the same layer, which enables climatic control, spatial organisation and scenery construction to operate simultaneously. All the related elements can be identified as what may be called the 'multi-screen'. The multi-screen separates, defines and organises space, taking the form of walls, partitions, windows, doors or furniture. It transforms the initial sheer volume into a rich complex of sub-spaces. Hence, the whole forms a system of five layers: site, access, structure, multi-screen and services.

The multi-screen endows the otherwise homogeneous structure and open space with spatial characteristics, climatic benefits and personalised expression. Defining and constructing scenery at the same time, it creates comfort and intimacy, as well as beauty and joy. The interior defined by the multi-screen is visually and environmentally divided, but aurally and psychologically connected, hence often leading to intricate spaces and hierarchical atmospheres. Its multiplied and responsive interface, echoing everyday banality and abundance, is beyond time and location.

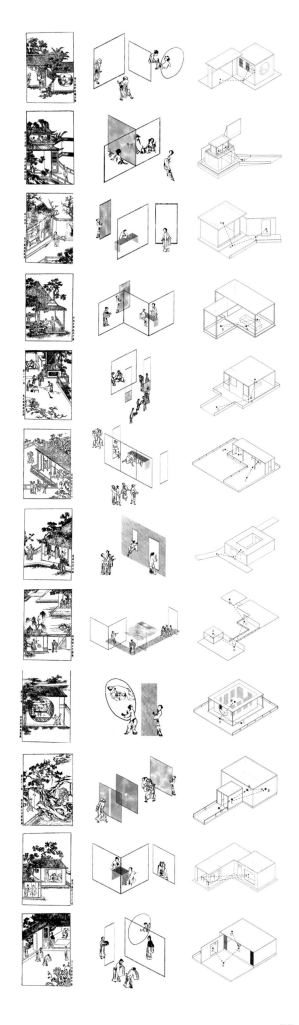

LanD Studio,
Typological analysis of the multi-screen,
2017

Twelve sets of intricate spatial relationships created by screens of various forms, sizes, positions and interrelations. The analysis is drawn from the scenes of the famous Chinese erotic novel *The Golden Lotus* (1708), in which the interplay of intimacy and voyeurism is a constant theme.

New Life for a Historical Urban Typology

Refurbishment, renovation and renewal of historical urban fabric is a constant theme in contemporary Chinese architectural practice. Architects are enthusiastic to explore this field. Recent projects have exhibited many effective strategies, such as taking advantage of ceiling height to insert a mezzanine, adding linings to improve insulation, replacing the original roof to add another storey, making use of the courtyard to densify, or rebuilding but still retaining the courtyard-house configuration. The common thread is to continuously conceive this urban typology not as a complete whole for external admiration, but as an inner world of unified parts for dynamic day-to-day activities.

Among many examples in Beijing, Institute for Provocation (IFP) refurbished a dilapidated siheyuan into a mixture of workplace and artists' residences, completed in 2013. The original reception room with lavish lattice screens was opened up into a shared studio, pertinent for the purpose of mutual exchange. ZAO/Standardarchitecture positively accepted the 'changed' condition by collective users over time and took it as the starting point of the 'Micro-Yuaner' renewal project (2014), a children's library and

IFP is a Beijing-based workspace and think-tank
hosting workshops, lectures and residencies. The
outward-looking IFP studio occuples the three south-
facing rooms, while the inward principal room and
wing room are temporary living spaces for foreign
artists working in China for short periods.

Institute for Provocation (IFP),
Workspace at Black Sesame Hutong,
Beijing,
2013

The original reception rooms of the house with lavish
lattice screens were combined into a shared studio.
This versatile space is suitable for a range of activities
such as creative work, hosting exhibitions, film
screenings and banquets.

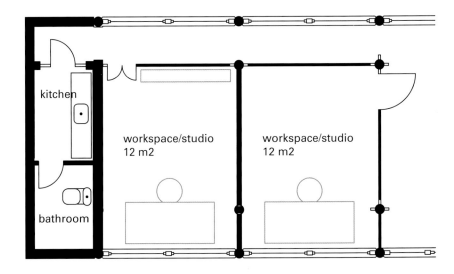

kitchen

bathroom

workspace/studio
12 m2

workspace/studio
12 m2

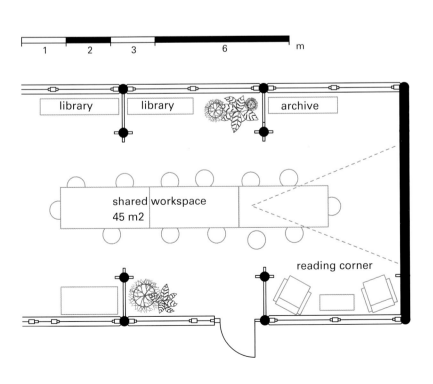

| 1 | 2 | 3 | 6 | m |

library | library | archive

shared workspace
45 m2

reading corner

Shown here before renovation, the site was a typical *dazayuan* – big messy courtyard – occupied and shared by a dozen families for the past fifty years. Each family built a small extended kitchen or storage space in the courtyard, which is usually considered as urban scrap and is cleared out during renovation.

Ke Zhang / ZAO /
standardarchitecture, Micro-
Yuan'er, Cha'er Hutong, Beijing,
2014

By redesigning, renovating and reusing the add-on structures in the hutong courtyard, the project demonstrates new possibilities of putting the messy additions to good use. Micro-Yuan'er received the Aga Khan Award for Architecture in 2016.

art centre where unexpected use of space was recognised as a critical layer of urban life and translated into a formal language. In 2015, TAO (Trace Architecture Office) rebuilt a set of four rental studio apartments on a tiny plot, reinterpreting the inward-facing courtyard-house relationship. Titled Split Courtyard House (*Sifenyuan*) – in contrast to the traditional 'unity courtyard house' (*siheyuan*), to suggest the transformation of social structure and lifestyle – it employs experimental construction methods such as a prefabricated lightweight wall panel system.

Reinventing the patrimony of multi-screen adaptability – superior secondary space-making and environment-mediating elements connected to a principal framework – can shed new light on the growing concerns of reintroducing time as a crucial dimension to architecture. An articulated hierarchy of territory and finely moderated surroundings can accommodate a wide range of activities. The inherent attributes of a historical urban typology can be extracted and reinvented. This powerful instrument may well take on a fresh look incorporating new materials and information technology, such as lightweight, airtight and soundproofing materials, digital panels, or even a non-solid shield of liquid or air. The hybrid, synthetic and ambiguous nature of multi-screen may pioneer plenty of novel design possibilities. To embrace architecture as an active and flexible organism is to abandon the obsessively purist ideal of architecture as resistance to the unexpected and to change. ⚙

Notes
1. Adrian Forty, *Words and Buildings: A Vocabulary of Modern Architecture*, Thames & Hudson (London), 2000, p 142.
2. John Habraken, *Supports: An Alternative to Mass Housing*, Architectural Press (London), 1972.
3. Stephen Kendall and Jonathan Teicher, *Residential Open Building*, Taylor and Francis (London), 1999.
4. Shiqing Zhang, 'From Curtain Furnishing to Xiao-Mu Furnishing: A Thread in the Evolution of Ancient Interior', *Interior Design & Decoration*, 6, 2001, pp 70–71.
5. Gottfried Semper, *The Four Elements of Architecture and Other Writings* (1851), trans Harry F Mallgrave and Wolfgang Herrmann, Cambridge University Press (Cambridge), 1989.
6. Francis Duffy, 'Measuring Building Performance', *Facilities*, 5, 1990, pp 17–22.
7. Stewart Brand, *How Buildings Learn: What happens After They're Built*, VIKING (New York), 1994.
8. Bernard Leupen, *Frame and Generic Space: A Study into the Changeable Dwelling Proceeding from the Permanent*, 010 Publishers (Rotterdam), 2006.

Li Hua / TAO
(Trace Architecture Office),
Split Courtyard House,
Hutong near White Pagoda Temple,
Beijing,
2015

The entrance sequence is from room to yard, instead of from yard to room in the traditional pattern, responding to the change from collective to individual occupancy. Although the yard is here the most private place, it retains its function as the living core, adhering to the Chinese enthusiasm for living with nature.

Jingxiang Zhu

Constructing Critically

Prefabricated Systems with Soul

Prefabrication is an obvious solution for the building needs of remote, economically deprived or disaster-stricken regions. But must it mean soulless standardisation? Certainly not – as the AIIA (Architecture Integration and Innovation Association) team at the Chinese University of Hong Kong has demonstrated. The team's leader, architect and associate professor **Jingxiang Zhu**, explains how they have developed flexible, easy-to-erect prefabricated systems that can adapt successfully to different settings and programmes, providing spaces that are not only functional, comfortable and resilient but also stimulating and even playful.

AIIA research team,
CUHK,
Grameen Bank,
Lukou village,
Xuzhou,
Jiangsu province,
China,
2014

The steel 'letter wall' at the southeast entrance of the Grameen Bank spells out 'Grameen China' in Chinese. The building, constructed with the New Bud System, adapts a double-pitched roof which is commonly found in the local village.

Wooden buildings in the gardens of Suzhou, log farmhouses in Yunnan, post-and-tie dwellings in Sichuan, and quickly assembled temporary shelters made of bamboo in contemporary Hong Kong – there are plenty of vernacular building types and products in China. However, in the minds of Chinese practitioners of the past three decades they are either too perfect to evolve, or too old to save.

China has held the record for the fastest-developing major country for years. Construction is going on at an unprecedented pace. Unfortunately, while using half of the world's concrete and a third of the world's steel, the design industry has not been contributing much on building integration, system invention or the definition of new issues.

Modern pioneers unveiled very broad potentials of the vernacular tradition. Konrad Wachsmann started from traditional wooden construction and shifted his research to sophisticated metal joints which are critical to rapid assembly and mass production. Frank Lloyd Wright designed affordable Usonian houses during the Great Depression. Jean Prouvé explored structures in plywood and aluminium, presenting his solution for the housing shortage after the Second World War. At the same time, Richard Buckminster Fuller extended his concern to the planet and invented new habitats for humankind. However, none of these experiments that originated from innovators' insight were responding to the actual needs of the time and place.

With a focus on buildings that serve the community, the AIIA (Architecture Integration and Innovation Association) research team at the Chinese University of Hong Kong (CUHK) – comprising professors, PhD researchers, designers, charity supporters and manufacturers – has been examining radical challenges in contemporary China: construction without quality control, income inequality, environmental pollution, lack of social security etc. It has produced experimental solutions to extreme projects, based on its members' long-term research on building systems and customised prefabrication.

Unlike the classical avant-garde's claim to the 'new', these experimental projects – a selection of which are presented below – have a non-theoretical, reconciliatory quality: the precarious but natural relationship between the experimental, industrial and regional directions. The built works are testimony to the fact that the intelligence of the constructional concepts and their regional adaptability are surprisingly parallel, as long as design knowhow and financial resources are concentrated towards the critical issues.

The New Bud System
After the catastrophic 2008 Sichuan earthquake, a barrack building type commonly used on construction sites was erected widely to accommodate large numbers of refugees, because of its rapid assembly. However, its very poor thermal performance did not allow people to use it as a long-term habitat.

This prompted me – with some assistance from a PhD student at CUHK and an engineer friend – to devise the 'New Bud System'. A strong composite system, it keeps the light-gauge steel frame of the barrack-type buildings but replaces their filling material with structural insulated panels (SIP), using a diaphragm effect and eliminating most diagonal braces or rods. SIP cuts off all thermal bridges and guarantees indoor comfort in both winter and summer. The New Bud System can be prefabricated in a factory, transported over a long distance and rapidly constructed on site with unskilled workers, while the design restriction has been reduced to a minimum.

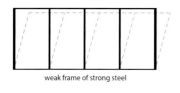

weak frame of strong steel

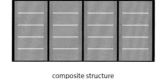

composite structure

careful opening distribution

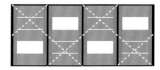

hidden path of internal force

strong wall of weak infill panel

Jingxiang Zhu,
New Bud System structural diagram,
2008

The structural diagram explains how the post framework with panel elements addresses seismic forces. Openings and surface skin are also distributed according to structural considerations.

AIIA (Architecture Integration and Innovation Association) research team, Chinese University of Hong Kong (CUHK), Mcedo Beijing School, Dali, Nairobi, Kenya, 2014

A classroom interior. The foldable steel structure of the frame system appears as 'inverted Y' columns.

After applying the New Bud System in a school reconstruction project with standard barrack form for a quake area in 2009, the CUHK team – which officially became AIIA in 2010 – continued to customise the design in subsequent projects, to demonstrate the system's potential for various programmes or site conditions.

A remote village, Dazu, at an altitude of 2,600 metres (8,500 feet) in a mountainous region on the southern border of Sichuan province, that is home to a minority ethnic group, became the second site for the system's application. With a simple timber-trellis cladding design, this modern building blends in with the rural ambiance of the log dwellings.

AIIA research team, CUHK,
Dazu Study Hall, Dazu village,
Yanyuan county, Sichuan province,
China, 2010

Viewed here from the ground to the southeast, the red mass of this second 'New Bud System' school stands out from its surroundings. The shelves on either side of the windows provide an illusion of a heavy wall. Although a lightweight structure, it feels like a castle to the local students.

With a simple timber-trellis cladding design, this modern building blends in with the rural ambiance of the log dwellings.

Seen from an elevated viewpoint, the flat building merges with the nearby farmhouses, respecting the mountains beyond.

The glass partitions define the classrooms, ensure sound insulation and allow light to be diffused, enriching the interior spatial experience.

Multipurpose space at the second floor. The large glass viewing panel at the right facing east allows sunshine to enter in the morning. The circular holes are specially designed vents for adjustable natural ventilation.

The 260-square-metre (2,800-square-foot) single-storey structure compactly houses three classrooms and a reading space, without wasting any space on corridors. All four areas are uniquely designed with different sizes, proportions and orientations, giving students a clear sense of location. Teachers can also make good use of the space by adjusting the doors.

Translucent partition walls are used to block noise, without hindering light penetration. Skylights help to light up areas far from the windows. Vents are well positioned and the stack effect is manipulated carefully to keep indoor space cool in summer and warm in winter.

Shelves near windows give the illusion of a heavy wall. This 'heavy' and modern school is a 'castle' in the mental world of the elementary students. Actually it is a very lightweight structure with a wall thickness of 16 centimetres (6 inches) and weight only one quarter that of a typical building with the same volume. The Study Hall has earthquake resistance up to the top intensity level of X (extreme shaking) on the Mercalli Intensity Scale. Over 90 per cent of the components are prefabricated in factories, reducing the time taken to assemble the superstructure to only 14 days. Skilful workers, teachers and volunteers erected the building in the rainy season of summer 2010. With a low construction cost, this project demonstrates an ideal option for buildings in areas threatened by natural disasters or stricken areas needing reconstruction.

After several other successful charity school projects and work stations for national nature reserves, the AIIA team was invited in November 2014 to build the office of Grameen Bank in the village of Lukou, Jiangsu province. The commission came from the Yunus China Centre, founded by Professor Muhammad Yunus – a banker and economist from Bangladesh who was awarded the 2006 Nobel Peace Prize – who had launched the 'Grameen China Project', supervising Chinese finance companies to operate in accordance with Yunus's social enterprise model.

In a blend of hand craft and industrial production, or low tech and high tech respectively, the villagers assembled the new building with simple tools.

The two-storey, 220-square-metre (2,400-square-foot) building not only provides office space for rural financial operations, but accommodates multiple activities such as gathering, performing, exhibiting and training. Together with outdoor space available to the villagers, this building became a true centre for Lukou village.

The building adapted volumetric forms commonly found in rural areas of northern Jiangsu province, but was built in a brand-new way: through well-organised distributed manufacturing. Large factories, small workshops and village builders all contributed to the component and material supply. Ninety per cent of the expenditure remained inside Jiangsu province. In a blend of hand craft and industrial production, or low tech and high tech respectively, the villagers assembled the new building with simple tools. Laymen and women from the village worked happily with the professional builders and university experts.

The thermally insulated surfaces with precisely designed openings guarantee winter insulation and summer ventilation. Equipped with a warm water supply and shower devices, this building also exemplifies an affordable rural dwelling prototype.

Checkered Playrooms

Dou Pavilion brought prefab building technology and its social impact to the forefront of the 2016 Venice Biennale. It was one of the few buildings in the exhibition that were built on a 1:1 scale to their original models, and became an important spot in Venice's Arsenale. Components of the wood pavilion were manufactured in mainland China, packed carefully and shipped to Venice. The precision in its design enabled it to be assembled on site within three days.

The pavilion originated in another recent project, a kindergarten model built in China's Gansu province, which had been adapted to the Mediterranean climate and shipping requirements. The model is composed of concave and convex squares, both inside and out, which create a fluctuant interface for visitors to discover individual relations with the structure.

Since 2015, a number of these structures, known also as Checkered Playrooms, were assembled by the AIIA team in remote villages in Gansu, in collaboration with the Western Sunshine Rural Development Foundation, to promote basic preschool education for more than 5,000 children between ages two and six. In the rural areas of the western provinces in China, thousands of children have insufficient pre-education facilities, as well as too few teachers. The Checkered Playrooms are intended to attract more teachers to these areas and provide modern facilities for the children.

The playful design makes these playrooms a hit with their users. Children enjoy hanging out in them, even without any toys. Different from traditional classroom design, the 'boxes' on the walls and on the floor are made child-friendly, and the children always love to sit or lie in these boxes and to explore other ways to occupy the spaces. Spatial exploration in the playrooms has become an important supplement to the original school curriculum, because it has proved to be helpful to the children's physical and mental development.

Equally significant is the playrooms' impact on community building. The components of the structure were made so light and user-friendly that assembling the buildings created opportunities to involve members of the local community and bring them together. By spring 2018, more than 110 playrooms had been built in various places in mainland China.

AIIA research team,
CUHK,
Checkered Playroom,
Huining,
Gansu province,
China,
2015

The first Checkered Playroom in Gansu province. The geometry offers an interesting comparison to nearby traditional buildings.

Agile Development

The CUHK AIIA team has been working on prefab lightweight constructions for a decade and has developed a group of prototypes which have been applied successfully in various projects in mainland China and overseas. To work with restricted resources or at extreme locations, the structure has to be robust but flexible, allowing it to be manufactured, packed, moved, mounted and jointed modularly. In addition to this, it should finally present sensual, haptic features such as the warmth of the material or its sculptural, tectonic quality. Such bipolar demands can be fulfilled exclusively through 'constructing critically' – a method embracing system integration, understanding of the vernacular, seeking out and planning resources, and iterative evolution.

In parallel with open and decisive dialogue between professionals and clients, the construction challenge and the agenda on necessity have navigated the team to a point of clarity in each individual project, regardless of the chaotically ever-changing reality of the vast developing areas. These applied projects and collected data consistently demonstrate a distinctive approach that moves away from the common trends of inefficient, energy-consuming, little-or-no-design and environment-disturbing building practices. As the result of a few human interventions, these works also outline the role of practice in a larger scope – a critical role played again and again, from historical master builders to the pioneers of the Modern Movement. ᗡ

AIIA research team,
CUHK,
Dou Pavilion,
Venice,
Italy,
2016

A variant of the Checkered Playroom – 'Dou Pavilion', the China outdoor pavilion for the 15th Venice Biennale of Architecture.

AIIA research team,
CUHK, Spatial Panel System,
Checkered Playroom,
Chongqing,
China,
2017

There are now more than 80 Checkered Playrooms in China, located over eight provinces. This is the fourth generation in Chongqing, constructed by volunteer secondary-students and their parents.

People's Architecture Office (PAO),
Mr Wang's Plugin House,
Guangzhou,
Guangdong province,
2017

Mr Wang's Plugin House took a handful of people just
one day to build. Mr Wang commissioned this Plugin House
to sit next to his expanding organic farming business.
He moved from the city to the countryside with the aim
of raising his newborn child away from an urban setting.

Plugin

Bridging the Gap Between Approaches to

James Shen

Society

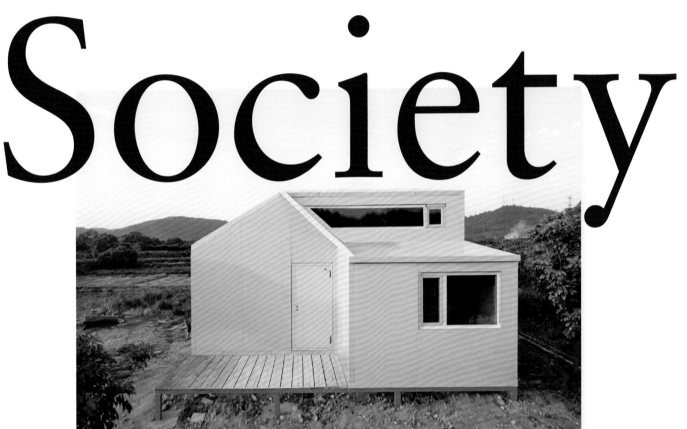

Top-Down and Bottom-Up Urban Development

Devising an urban regeneration strategy that is low cost and boldly modern yet pleasing to preservationists and non-disruptive to residents sounds like an impossible goal. Yet the multidisciplinary Beijing practice People's Architecture Office (PAO) have achieved it with their modular system Plugin. Mass-customisable and adaptable to a multitude of uses and scales, it has already been deployed in a range of settings across China. PAO co-founder **James Shen** tells the story of how it works and how it was developed – through a combination of government support and close input from clients.

China's unique context has fostered a culture of experimentation that occurs from the top down and the bottom up. Continuous waves of sweeping socioeconomic reforms have shaped the country's tumultuous history and its urban and rural development. On the ground, and often through informal means, people are forced to quickly adapt to rapid urban growth, rising costs and pressure to relocate.

People's Architecture Office's Plugin system responds to these complex forces from a position between government and local residents. First deployed as a government-supported urban regeneration pilot in Dashilar, a hutong district in the centre of historic Beijing, it is a method of upgrading deteriorating urban conditions without destroying existing buildings or relocating local residents. The success of the pilot has since led to the development of other Plugin projects across China that range in type, use and location.

People's Architecture Office,
PAO Office Courtyard House Plugin,
Dashilar,
Beijing,
2015

PAO moved its offices to Dashilar in 2015 to work more closely with residents and local authorities to deploy the Plugin system. The office renovation, the largest Plugin project at the time, was a trial run for many of the techniques that were later used in other Plugin projects.

People's Architecture Office (PAO),
Mrs Dong's Courtyard House Plugin,
Dashilar,
Beijing,
2015

Mrs Dong's apartment underwent a drastic transformation, as seen in these before and after photos of the interior.

People-Centred Design

In 2014, PAO began observing the daily concerns of Dashilar's residents first-hand. The office gained a deep understanding of their physical and social circumstances, and only then determined the issues it could engage with more effectively. In 2015, the architects moved their office to Dashilar, fully embedding themselves within the neighbourhood.

That same year Mrs Dong became the first local resident to commission a Plugin. A woman in her 50s, she was living with her son in a cramped 15-square-metre (160-square-foot) space. Her home is a subdivided unit belonging to a degrading traditional courtyard house that is shared with other residents. Renovations would normally encompass the entirety of the structure and thus a complicated process of negotiation among all of the neighbours. Furthermore, Mrs Dong and other residents of Dashilar fear relocation, and because of this uncertainty feel little incentive to invest in their own homes.

With Mrs Dong's concerns in mind, PAO designed the Plugin system in order to build a new house inside her existing one. Named the Courtyard House Plugin, the structure stands independently from the old building that envelops it, and therefore does not affect adjacent units. The Plugin is built using modular parts that can be easily assembled and disassembled. Mrs Dong has limited means, but invested in the Plugin because she views it as a physical asset that can be taken with her and rebuilt were she forced to relocate.

Mrs Dong's Plugin provided a significant upgrade to her living conditions. The leaky house was difficult to heat, especially during the winter. The Plugin Panel system has superior insulation, increasing the energy efficiency of the original house tenfold, while the large windows bring more light into the deep interior, significantly improving natural ventilation. An unexpected outcome of the renovation was the increase in interior space: in order to clean crumbling plaster off her floors in her original house, Mrs Dong kept furniture away from the flaking walls. The Plugin allowed her to move her belongings against the panel walls.

People's Architecture Office (PAO),
Courtyard House Plugin,
Dashilar,
Beijing,
2014

One of two early Plugins that were inserted into subdivisions of existing courtyard houses. Mrs Dong, the first local resident to commission a Plugin, is seen in front of her own apartment before her renovation.

Social Aesthetics

PAO's Plugin is an experiment in atypical aesthetics in the context of the hutongs. By maintaining a split between old and new, it makes it unnecessary to alter existing structures. This unusual visual contrast has had palpable social and political reactions. The aesthetic innovation of the Plugin, in other words, is its ability to relate to parties of disparate interests. Preservationists often take a hard line and push for historic buildings to be renovated to an 'original' state with little regard for the people living in such structures. They can, however, appreciate how the Plugin leaves original buildings intact. For local inhabitants, the dilapidated structures are stigmatised as housing for the poor. Indifferent to preservation, residents are more concerned with improving living conditions. With the Plugin they are content to keep old buildings because it does not conflict with the improvement of their quality of life; in fact it makes upgrading easier. Finally, government officials, who usually champion renovations in a historic but sanitised style, tolerate the mismatch between the old and the new because of the Plugin's practicality and the support from residents as well as academics. Government officials had not previously been aware of other alternatives to upgrading that did not involve demolishing buildings and relocating people. The aesthetic of the Plugin is therefore a manifestation of the intersection of complex social, political and cultural forces.

Technology for Social Impact

Mrs Dong's Plugin is one of several dozen Plugin projects built across China. Begun as an experimental architectural project, the design has developed into a mass-produced product and building system. PAO follows up with Plugin clients, many of whom live in the same neighbourhood as the practice's office, as a way to learn from mistakes and improve on the system. A process spanning many years, this incremental approach has resulted in a wide array of uses, types and scales. Plugins range from single-storey houses such as Mrs Dong's to the People's Station cultural centre, a 400-square-metre (4,300-square-foot) multistorey mixed-use building in Yantai, Shandong province, completed in 2017.

People's Architecture Office (PAO),
Mrs Fan's Plugin House,
Changchun Jie,
Beijing,
2016

Mrs Fan's Plugin House was the first Plugin to be commissioned as an external addition. Recently married and expecting her first child, she wanted to move out of her parents' new apartment on the outskirts of Beijing and back to the hutong neighbourhood where she was born. For Mrs Fan, the Plugin House was a rare housing option that was affordable and had the modern amenities she was accustomed to.

People's Architecture Office (PAO),
People's Station,
Yantai,
Shandong province,
2017

The People's Station is a 400-square-metre (4,300-square-foot) multistorey cultural centre, and one of the largest structures to use the Plugin system. The external steel framework permits Plugin Panels to be added or subtracted without affecting the structure, allowing for spatial flexibility on each floor of the building.

It is rare that a design office can work directly with low-income people like Mrs Dong. Through the economy of scale, PAO has used mass production to reduce the cost of construction by up to 50 per cent, making high-quality housing affordable to disadvantaged communities. The panellised system is injection-moulded and integrates structural connections during production to further reduce cost. A house can be built in one day with one tool using a handful of unskilled labourers. Panels are flat-packed and shipped economically. On arrival they are light enough to be hand-carried and small enough to weave through the narrow alleys of the hutongs, little doorways and hard-to-reach locations, such as the interior of Mrs Dong's house.

The Plugin system is also an example of mass customisation. Adjustable moulds are used to produce customised and standard Plugin Panel modules that can be assembled to conform to the unique conditions of each site. The flexibility of the system is apparent from its broad range of applications. Plugins have been constructed inside buildings, adjacent to them, on top and detached from them, in historical districts, urban villages and rural areas.

People's Architecture Office (PAO),
Plugin House,
Shangwei,
Shenzhen,
Guangdong province,
2017

A number of Plugins have been built in the urban village of Shangwei within the ruins of abandoned properties, the owners of which cannot be located. Government authorities are interested in upgrading these properties for reuse without affecting the original structure, at least until there is more clarity regarding ownership.

Innovation Through Public Engagement

The development of the Plugin system relied on events such as Beijing Design Week and the Bi-City Biennale of Urbanism/Architecture in Shenzhen, which brought together architects and local authorities in search of creative approaches to pressing urban issues. PAO has leveraged these opportunities to test and demonstrate ideas in areas such as Dashilar and the urban villages of Yantian and Shangwei in Shenzhen, where local governments have relaxed regulation and supplied funding and support for early-stage development.

The projects completed since the Dashilar pilot helped visitors understand the architects' unusual approach, attracting residents willing to fund their own Plugins. This demand from ordinary clients subsequently resulted in the development of alternative Plugin types and uses, enabling PAO to test out viable markets. The work has also attracted investment for the testing and certification of the Plugin system as a formal product recognised within a national building regulation framework.

The Plugin system is the culmination of years of intimate engagement with residents and officials in the specific political and social setting of Dashilar. It is through this rigorous and demanding process that it has developed into a robust system. Begun as small architectural insertions, Plugins have evolved into large multistorey structures. The system is adapting to the challenges of different sites and locations, and proving its viability in a wider range of contexts. ⌂

Everyday Change and the Unrecognisable System

Xiahong Hua and Shen Zhuang

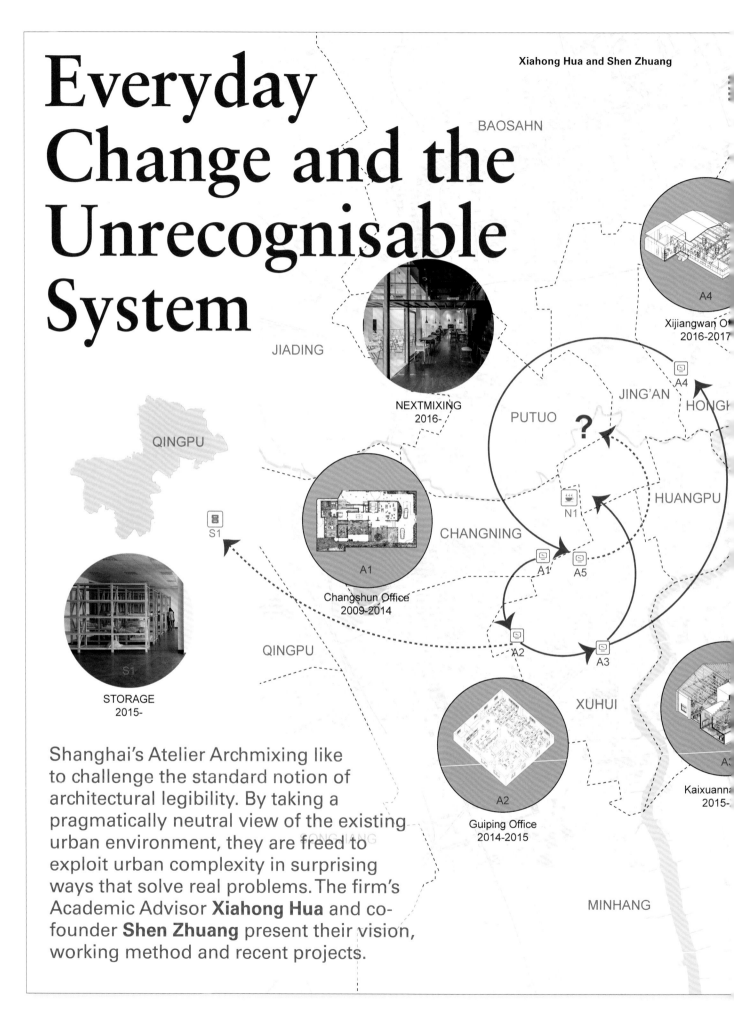

BAOSAHN

JIADING

NEXTMIXING
2016-

QINGPU

PUTUO

JING'AN

HONG

?

A4

Xijiangwan O
2016-2017

CHANGNING

HUANGPU

N1

S1

A1

A5

Changshun Office
2009-2014

A1

STORAGE
2015-

QINGPU

A2

A3

XUHUI

A2

Guiping Office
2014-2015

Kaixuann:
2015-

MINHANG

Shanghai's Atelier Archmixing like to challenge the standard notion of architectural legibility. By taking a pragmatically neutral view of the existing urban environment, they are freed to exploit urban complexity in surprising ways that solve real problems. The firm's Academic Advisor **Xiahong Hua** and co-founder **Shen Zhuang** present their vision, working method and recent projects.

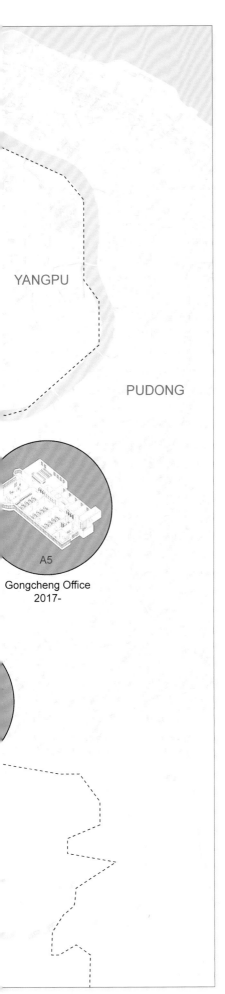

YANGPU

PUDONG

A5

Gongcheng Office
2017-

**Atelier Archmixing,
'New Year,
New Office' map,
Shanghai,
2014-18**

In 2014, failing to find a suitable long-term solution as its lease in an old downtown residence was coming to an end, the practice initiated a plan of annual moves. The 'New Year, New Office' programme calls for a workplace in a different region of Shanghai every year, with a concurrent urban research programme focused on the new area. The workplace was divided into two parts: storage in the suburbs (S1) and an office. In 2016 the office was further divided, into a nomadic design and research office (A2–A5) and a multifunctional gallery and cultural venue (N1) in the downtown area.

**Atelier Archmixing,
Gongcheng office,
Xuhui District,
Shanghai,
2017-**

This was the practice's fifth office, located near one of the city's busiest commercial centres. Punching holes in the walls of this former kindergarten turned separate classrooms into connected offices that were equipped with Archmixing-designed portable furniture. The pink walls, educational accessories and traces of the demolition were deliberately kept.

For Shanghai-based Atelier Archmixing, design practice is informed by a turn to the everyday. Since it was established in 2009, the studio has been concentrating on familiar, typical programmes in Shanghai and its neighbouring cities, towns and villages in the Yangtze River Delta. The majority of the projects have been small educational, commercial and community-service facilities with humble budgets, and the briefs have included partial interior or facade renovations for modest structures of a type not usually considered historically significant. Attention to everyday urbanism has proven a necessary and effective way of grasping the ever-changing essence of the region's built environment, and of developing homegrown design strategies in response.

New Year, New Office

In recent decades, Chinese cities such as Shanghai have undergone all manner of architectural change, from top-down development and renovation to informal, bottom-up construction and temporary installation. Since 2012, Atelier Archmixing has undertaken a series of urban studies in Shanghai, both independently and collaboratively, and these have contributed to the studio's belief that everyday transformations – large or small, glorious or banal – are not inconsequential to new practices, but rather a source of inspiration.

In 2014, unable to find a suitable new long-term space, the practice initiated a 'new year, new office' plan, moving its workplace to a different quarter of the city each year, meanwhile observing, experiencing and analysing everyday urbanism at the neighbourhood scale. To facilitate this programme, the studio was divided into three parts based on function and frequency of use. Storage is now hidden inexpensively in the suburbs; the seasonal exhibition and lecture venue is in the downtown area, where it realises economic independence as a flexible commercial space, and the main office is nomadic. The practice has so far transformed the functional and formal traces of five diverse spaces into suitable design studios. This constant seeking out, adapting, adjusting and reusing of different spaces has encouraged the architects to focus more on the interiors of both buildings and the cities in which they are set.[1] 'New year, new office' has been not only an experiment in one firm's positioning of itself within the city, but also a laboratory for cost-effective contextual design and the creation of an improvisatory, nomadic work culture.

Analytic Restoration

The studio's urban research focuses on utility and the requirements of living and how these are expressed in the built environment. The architects have found that changes in the everyday world encompass both adaptation to existing conditions and the application of realisable forms and readily available crafts and materials. Huangma Club (2017), a residential settlement in Shanghai, showcases what an informal construction can achieve both spatially and technologically in a leftover urban corner. In the practice's Hengfengli urban study (2017), the 260-metre (85-foot) long facade had acquired in the course of its living evolution countless structural and mechanical additions. To determine the divergences between current conditions and the original construction, the practice developed an approach called 'analytic restoration', which applies separate diagrams to the various supplements or alterations to the former structure. When classifying these items, according to either orthodox architectural categories or new, ad-hoc groupings, all elements, architectural and non-architectural (conventionally conceived), are accorded equal weight. Each contributes independently to an authentic living purpose, without the aggregate necessarily coalescing into a unified logic. Effectiveness is the only criterion.

Spatial Redundancy

In Chinese everyday urbanism, a part or fragment typically relies on a whole system to realise a practical goal. A balcony turns into a kitchen; a staircase supports a room; a roof is home to a magnificent pigeon coop. Such features are revealed, for example, in the firm's research on the 'One Half House' in Shanghai. Hidden in an ordinary residential area, its long linear structure is half dead, with bricks blocking the windows and doors, guarding against illegal occupation after the previous residents had moved

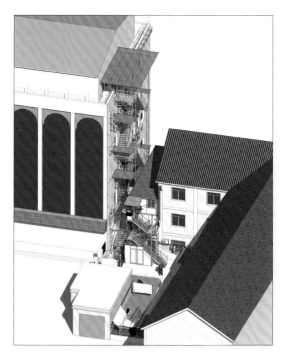

Atelier Archmixing,
Huangma Club urban study,
Tongxin Road,
Shanghai,
2017

An example of an informal, improvised construction, filling the 5.6-metre (18.4-foot) emergency-exit space between two old buildings. To reach the illegal rooftop hostel, a five-storey steel staircase was inserted, accompanied by a three-storey dormitory and its narrow stairs and slim corridors. The entrance yard was occupied by a shared laundry room. Hectic life covered all vertical and horizontal surfaces. Steel or plastic panels, furniture, housewares, domestic appliances and unidentifiable detritus – all were employed as building materials. Unfortunately, the club was demolished soon after the practice's investigation

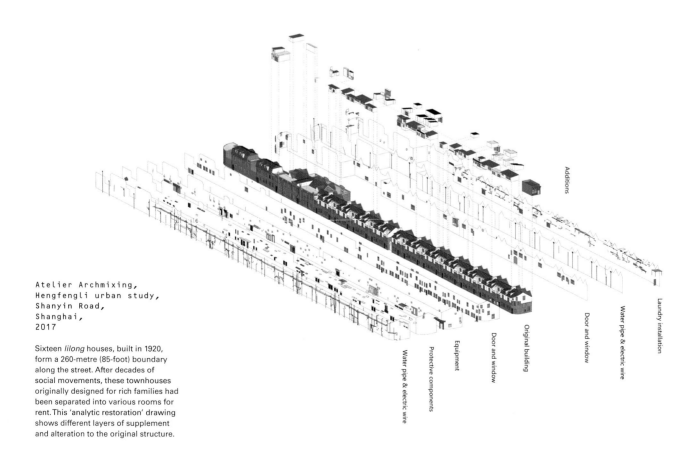

Atelier Archmixing,
Hengfengli urban study,
Shanyin Road,
Shanghai,
2017

Sixteen *lilong* houses, built in 1920, form a 260-metre (85-foot) boundary along the street. After decades of social movements, these townhouses originally designed for rich families had been separated into various rooms for rent. This 'analytic restoration' drawing shows different layers of supplement and alteration to the original structure.

Water pipe & electric wire

Protective components

Equipment

Door and window

Original building

Door and window

Water pipe & electric wire

Laundry installation

Additions

out. Due to structural, economic and social reasons, the other half, with all its surface additions, including air conditioners, laundries and plants, is still functioning and busy with residents. Here, the unused part can be seen as an extreme example of 'spatial redundancy',[2] such that the modification, accumulation, repetition, superabundance, residue and dislocation of material spaces and cultural symbols is not assessed negatively, as 'remnant' or 'superfluous'. Impure, inefficient and imperfect sites are not necessarily harmful; rather, they are inevitable. In the field of information technology, unused spaces and redundancy are harnessed for error correction and to avoid critical failure; similarly, by the firm's thinking, in the urban built environment, spatial redundancy uncovers complexity and contradiction, especially in developing regions such as China, and reserves otherwise unvalued aspects of the everyday for the future city.

Seen through a historical lens, 'spatial redundancy' reflects the evolution of living spaces. It encourages architects to reconsider what 'interior' – of both buildings and the city – means for future architecture. Interior has long been underestimated in the architectural field, as secondary and not as essential as the exterior. Nevertheless, in a well-developed and constantly changing world, as a space directly interacts with real life, its interior becomes the primary space within which architects can operate. Layer upon layer, the accumulation of the inner surfaces of diverse components results in a new architecture. In the urban context, alleys are commonly encountered that have been gradually built up from various architectural or structural fragments and domestic items: gates and doors, steps, platforms, drying racks, bicycle shelters, canopies, outdoor furniture and even mop buckets can constitute the urban interior, such that no boundary divides public life from private.

According to the systematic thinking embedded in classical and modern architecture, change is meaningful, and, if positive, progressive. By contrast, Atelier Archmixing maintains that all buildings are in a temporary state of present usage. The urban context is constituted of successive 'independent' moments, and the extant spaces from other times, with their divergent origins and features, are akin to the varied life forms simultaneously coexisting on earth.

The Unrecognisable System

To challenge the established 'Recognisable System' in mainstream academic thinking, which values architectural phenomena and design canons with legible features and obvious sources, Atelier Archmixing has coined a new term, the 'Unrecognisable System',[3] to signify architectural instances with opaque origins and hybrid qualities. The Unrecognisable System is a theoretical understanding/reading of the existing built environment, as well as a foundation for future design practice. It advocates taking the urban context as a neutral background, applying all kinds of concepts, forms and techniques without prejudice to meet new utilitarian requirements, using and mixing these flexibly, and liberating them from their origins and inherited meanings.

The Unrecognisable System describes both an attitude to design and a methodology. On the one hand, it views the current situation, whether natural or artificial, as neutral; on the other it means never to privilege a new intervention or a contemporary idea over a common tradition. For instance, Olion Kindergarten (2017) was a commission to renovate a former community centre, used only for five years, into a day nursery in an emerging suburban area of

Shanghai. The designers took the banal three-storey building as a neutral platform instead of a final spatial and structural order. The maximum number of classrooms with standard facility units was inserted in a conventional column-and-beam system, but distinctive characteristics achieved with the introduction of double spaces and scales, and the shaping of the 2.25-metre (7.38-foot) high suspended ceilings to form the dominant scale, creating a little world. Scattered boxes, vertical or inclined, solid or transparent, colourful or white, cut through the lower level to touch the structural ceiling 3.5 to 4.5 metres (11.5 to 14.8 feet) high. The resulting houses-in-a-house, like spatial nesting dolls, helped to achieve diversity within standard rooms. All equipment was exposed equally, as building elements. Old and new structures and scales integrate, not only inside but also outside. Colourful squares painted alternately on the exterior surfaces were deliberately organised to obscure the former storey divisions. Using colour patterns to distinguish the renovated building from its surroundings was economical and effective; no change to the old architectural organisation, even of the windows, was needed.

Atelier Archmixing, Olion Kindergarten, Baoshan District, Shanghai, 2017

In an emerging suburban area, a former community centre in use for only five years was renovated as a kindergarten. A light steel zigzag gallery was added as an entrance path and a spatial division setting off the playground. Graphic patterns on the exterior economically and effectively obscure the storey divisions and distinguish the renovated building from its surroundings. No changes to the elevation, not even to the fenestration, were needed.

Two scale systems were applied within a conventional column-and-beam system. A 2.25-metre (7.38-foot) scale assembled from standard walls and big windows created an intimate world for the children. Between the lower ceiling and the structural one 3.5 to 4.5 metres (11.5 to 14.8 feet) high, scattered boxes – vertical or inclined, solid or transparent, colourful or white – provide diversity within classrooms of standard size and function.

Five urban facade renovations Atelier Archmixing completed from 2012 to 2017 illustrate well the firm's belief that the fragment matters to both everyday urbanism and new design.[4] One noteworthy example is the renovation for the Longhua Elder Care Center (2016), located in a dense residential area in downtown Shanghai. In this instance, a new building, with only the foundation completed, was redesigned. In the previous construction drawings, the plan was poorly arranged, with all rooms leading off the corridor and no public spaces, just like in a hospital. The corridor was dark, and the one balcony isolated and largely occupied by the air-conditioner. Initially, the only parts subject to the designers' intervention were the exterior walls, balconies and roofs. To explore the potential of these parts to humanise the daily lives of the residents, the architect persuaded the client to refocus the programme, from surface beautification to spatial reorganisation. Continuous balconies of varying sizes were built out from the exterior walls. All rooms were provided two public accesses. Some parts of the corridor were widened, and roof windows were added to improve illumination and ventilation. Glazed meeting rooms were installed on the empty roofs, where residents could watch television, play cards, chat or just sunbathe. These new communal spaces incorporate light and inexpensive structures and materials, in ways that reflect the informal additions and modifications widespread in the everyday surroundings. Whether from the perspective of the programme or the design strategy, such interventions are 'soft' and not easily categorised, but they are effective and efficient in solving functional problems. Moreover, such subtle changes are exactly where a true architectural identity resides.

Atelier Archmixing,
Lili House,
Suzhou,
Jiangsu province,
2012

An old workshop in the ancient town is surrounded by sloped-roof dwellings. The house is designed to be accessed from a narrow lane beside the gable wall rather than from the front yard. A walk along the canal, down the main street, through a dark lane and finally into the building offers an impressive experience of progressive enclosure within a traditional town environment.

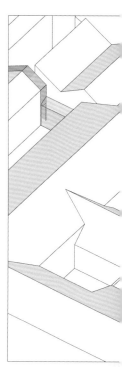

Atelier Archmixing,
Longhua Elder Care Center,
Xuhui District,
Shanghai,
2016

Continuous balconies of varying sizes were built out from the exterior walls, creating an open public space for formerly isolated rooms.

Public spaces from inexpensive structures and materials add light to the elevation and resemble the informal additions and modifications widespread in the surrounding everyday setting.

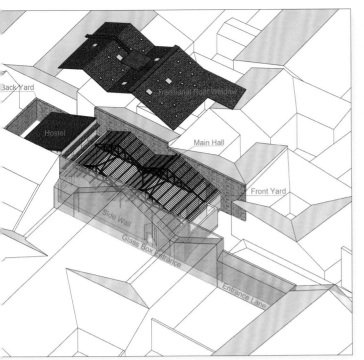

Forty traditional-style skylights lead to a 'hall' under the sloping roof and the sky. Walking out from a window and standing on the little platform, one is totally embraced by hills of grey tiles.

Design practice entails applying effective strategies and technologies to meet present demands rather than chasing revolutionary concepts, pure forms, novel materials or elaborate constructions.

The Unrecognisable System tends to break the boundaries between inside and outside, private and public. The Lili House (2012), a renovation and extension of an aged, plain workshop building in the ancient town of Suzhou in Jiangsu province, showcases Atelier Archmixing's insight into the architectural meaning of the interior, not only of the building, but also of the city. All around the structure, with its two adjoining gable roofs, are sloped-roof dwellings. The designer chose to access this single-storey house from a narrow lane beside the gable wall, rather than from the front yard. A walk along the town's canal, down its main street, through the dark entry lane and finally into the building offers an impressive experience of progressive interiorisation within a traditional town environment. Since the sloping roof is another interface with the surroundings, a small bridge was built to connect skylight and slope. When walking out onto it, one is totally embraced by hills of grey tiles. Under the roof, patchy sunlight penetrates through 40 traditional-style skylights that connect the otherwise gloomy inside with the blue sky. At one corner of the hall stands a diagonal glass-box entrance. When reaching the end of the dim back alley, a passer-by will encounter this bright portal, a kind of lamp onto the alley, and glimpse the private scene.

The Architecture of Change

Following years of urban studies and design practice, Atelier Archmixing advocates an 'architecture of change' fostered by the belief that the meaning of building is to provide a temporary vessel for ever-changing life. As a dynamic process, the building incorporates a continuously evolving set of objectives, strategies and actions; it is not its own end, as a design product or artistic creation.

Architectural change is not synonymous with progress or innovation. Design practice entails applying effective strategies and technologies to meet present demands rather than chasing revolutionary concepts, pure forms, novel materials or elaborate constructions.

To a large extent, all architectural changes are equivalent. The system has no priority over the fragment; unity has no priority over parts; the exterior has no priority over the interior. For everyday urbanism, typical features are never monumental landmarks of permanence, but fragments of highly compressed space and time. In a region with a large population and rapid urbanisation such as China, a signature architectural performance is seldom around for long, whereas utilitarian efficiency is ever more urgent and pragmatic.[5] ⌂

Notes
1. Zhuang Shen and Hua Xiahong, 'Work Within the City', *Time+Architecture*, 5, 2015, pp 100–07.
2. Zhuang Shen and Hua Xiahong, 'Spatial Redundancy', *Time+Architecture, op cit*, pp 108–11.
3. Zhuang Shen and Hua Xiahong, 'Everyday Change, Unrecognizable System', in *New Architecture* 6, 2014, pp 16–19.
4. Hua Xiahong and Zhuang Shen, 'On Façade Renovation', *Time+Architecture*, 4, 2016, pp 24–8.
5. This paper was funded by the National Natural Science Foundation of China programme 'Study on Design Strategies of Ordinary Building Renewal Based on the Everyday Efficiency of Urban Space' (No 51778419).

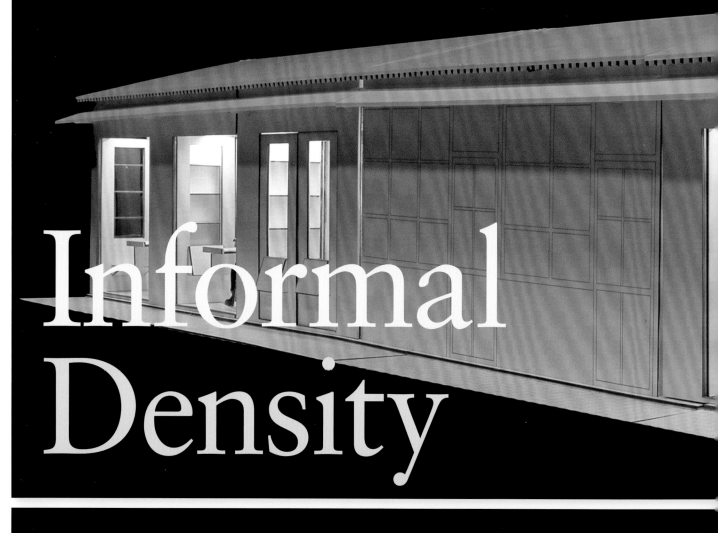

Informal Density

Animating Historical Neighbourhoods

Hui Wang

URBANUS,
Home for the Craftsmen,
Dashilar,
Beijing,
2015

The design creates multiple modes of spatial interfaces along the hutong alley for various types of social interactions.

Awareness of the value of historical neighbourhoods in China's cities is growing. But how can they be successfully integrated in forward-looking plans for urban development? URBANUS, a design practice and think-tank based in Beijing and Shenzhen, has been leading the way in finding architectural solutions to the country's urban challenges. **Hui Wang**, one of its co-founders, profiles URBANUS's approach through three recent projects that have injected new life, diversity and community cohesion into one of Beijing's hutong districts.

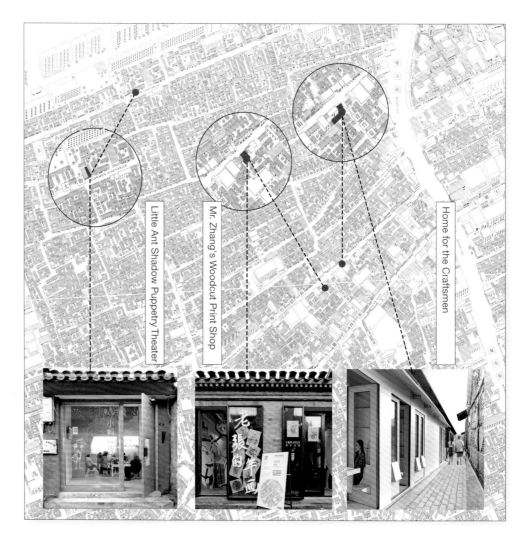

URBANUS,
'Informal density' project series,
Dashilar,
Beijing,
2013–15

Scattered around the Dashilar hutong area, the three small projects attempt to implant the 'informal density' of craftsmen within a demographically monotonous neighbourhood with the ambitious idea of revitalising a stagnated historical region by means of inside-out and bottom-up renewal strategies.

Little Ant Shadow Puppetry Theater

Mr. Zhang's Woodcut Print Shop

Home for the Craftsmen

Many historical neighbourhoods were sacrificed in the initial wave of China's urbanisation, but now they are often the first ones to be redeemed. Dashilar, an over-600-year-old district of hutongs (narrow streets) in the Qianmen area of Beijing, has gone through this sacrifice-to-redemption process during recent urban gentrification.

Over a decade ago, when historic preservation was still a vague concept among the public, high land value and low operational efficiency in this region naturally led to profit-driven developments, and a large-scale demolition plan to rebuild from scratch was underway. Fortunately, the ultra-high residential density and extremely complex landownership in this area made the demolition process far more difficult than expected. In the extended execution period, the call for preserving historical neighbourhoods gradually became a collective consensus, and the past tabula-rasa plan was criticised and dismissed. Meanwhile, the developer faced a dilemma: in the course of the demolition and resettlement, it had obtained many discrete land parcels, and these types of discontinuous properties were incompatible with its familiar formulas for large-scale area development. It needed a new vision. Consequently, the developer changed its strategy and brought forth the idea of soft, organic and redemptive renewal. In line with the context of the existing hutong fabric, the Dashilar hutong district's sustainable renewal was planned to be a neighbourhood that would mix the new with the old in a coexisting symbiosis. To achieve these objectives, the developer started to invite a variety of planners and designers through the platform of Beijing Design Week (BJDW) to explore new approaches to rehabilitate this historic area.

Since 2013, URBANUS has participated in the BJDW in consecutive years for the organic urban renewal programme in the Dashilar district with some small but strategic projects. These projects are designated as the office's theoretical proposition of 'informal density'.

URBANUS has noticed that, even if the physical environment is preserved, the overly monotonous demographic structure and business typology in an area will result in a rigid 'formal density' that may exacerbate the decline of the region. Therefore, it is important to adjust 'formal density' with 'informal density', which might otherwise be termed 'non-predominant density'. This approach will result in a diversity of population that will bring vitality into the neighbourhood, introduce variations for its future evolution, and even trigger 'genetic mutations' in the system. Thus, the urban system is revived from inside out and bottom up, as the 'informal density' is not merely a catalyst, but also a reactant participating in the 'chemical reactions' of the region. It will gradually renew the content of an urban system to achieve organic renewal in the end.

With the Dashilar hutong district, the specific 'informal density' that URBANUS seeks to introduce is the craftsman community. In Dashilar, once the most vivid commercial district of Beijing's south downtown, the population of craftsmen had been second to that of merchants in the old days, when their services were functionally indispensable for the city's daily life. It was only after the industrial and post-industrial periods that craftsmen became outdated, and craftsmanship became gentrified as a kind of artwork deviated from the everyday. The presentation of the work and life of the craftsman community in a residential district has disappeared, and the remaining craftsman community became hidden, marginalised and inactive.

One virtue of historical urban neighbourhoods lies in their charm and interest: interesting people with their interesting works and interesting lives. Unfortunately, nowadays in the Dashilar district, the real-estate value far exceeds its usage value, and this fact drives a growing number of property owners to leave for better residential districts and lease their houses to low-income migrants who merely help watch over their properties. Consequently, the exciting elements are gradually fading away from the neighbourhood, and it is becoming a lower-quality residential quarter. Thus, it is imperative to introduce valuable and sustainable trades and lifestyles to prevent the area from turning into a slum. Dashilar needs redemption from those developers who once advocated for the complete demolition of the old and its reconstruction from scratch. The discrete properties in their hands are the perfect resources for cultivating the 'informal density' to reboot the stagnated system. Under this circumstance, URBANUS began to search for new opportunities in this new development pattern. The practice invited the craftsmen as the 'informal density' to the existing social fabric, where their creative works contribute towards the vitality of the area, and transform their workplaces from passive costs into positive energy in transitioning the life of the neighbourhood.

Case One: Letting 'Informal Density' Appear
URBANUS's first attempt to implant 'informal density' started with BJDW in 2013. At that time, Yang Mei Zhu Diagonal Alley had just been redesigned by the developer, who offered its vacant stores as temporary showcases for local artisans. Mr Zhang, a woodcut print artist living and working quietly in the area, was identified. His studio was buried within a multi-family courtyard compound. With a storefront showcasing his artwork to the tourists on the main hutong alley, it would be a great opportunity for him to display his life and work to the community. However, such a design for a particular client was uncommon, since the Chinese approach to architectural commissions is normally aimed at abstract users and an abstract market, and architects seldom design for someone or something specific. For example, many new art galleries in China are visualised in the design phase as empty, with no collections, staff or visitors. URBANUS needed to learn how to acquaint themselves with their users first. Therefore, in designing this temporary shop, the architects spent a lot of time observing Zhang's life.

The practice invited the craftsmen as the 'informal density' to the existing social fabric, where their creative works contribute towards the vitality of the area, and transform their workplaces.

URBANUS,
Mr Zhang's Woodcut Print Shop,
Dashilar,
Beijing,
2013

Slogan cartoons pervade Mr Zhang's temporary
showroom, declaring manifestoes on the
organic rehabilitation of the old neighbourhood.

The final scheme relocated Zhang's unique worktable to the storefront so that visitors would see how his works were generated first hand. Centring around this worktable, slogan cartoons hung in mid-air, declaring design manifestos on the organic revival of the old neighbourhood. The artistic aura was reinforced by the flanking walls with murals of enlarged works by Zhang. This workshop atmosphere encouraged interactions between Zhang and visitors, where the craftsman could enjoy performing his craft as the visitors applauded in awe. As an experiment, this temporary showcase gave Zhang confidence in further anchoring his business in this area and affirmed the conviction that 'informal density' would bring much joy and life to the neighbourhood.

Case Two: Letting 'Informal Density' Be Respected

During the 2014 BJDW, URBANUS designed a small theatre for the Little Ant Shadow Puppetry Theatre on Xi He Yan Street. 'Little Ants' is the nickname for a group of adult artists with growth hormone deficiency (GHD), who not only look like but are also as tall as children. This shadow puppetry performance and production group is a self-improvement role model of the GHD community, proving that they can make a living just as much as the average adult can.

URBANUS sought to employ a contemporary architectural language to create a positive social image, provide a new public showcase for this particular group of people with disabilities, and integrate them into the community. On the ceiling, four layers of cut-out screens with shadow puppet patterns form a dramatic theatre space. A mirror on one flanking wall visually doubles the narrow space. The ultra-transparent storefront window – donated by the glass manufacturer who also provides the same product for Apple Store branches – exhibits the dramatic interior atmosphere to people passing by in the hutong. The stage, designed to be rotatable, leads to the backstage area, which double-functions as a workshop. To make maximum use of the space, which is only 2 metres (6.5 feet) wide, a curvilinear desk was designed to let these small actors sit on one side, while their director sits in the middle of the other side to guide their work. This beloved place for shadow puppetry performances, production and sales has quickly won the hearts of locals and has become a favourite after-school spot for children from the nearby primary school. The design generates a fresh image for the theatre and attracts many tourists to visit the neighbourhood. The project's success has proved that an attractive design can effectively help to implant 'informal density' within existing 'formal density'.

URBANUS,
Little Ant Shadow Puppetry Theatre,
Dashilar,
Beijing,
2014

right: The humble storefront of the Little Ant Shadow Puppetry Theatre set into a typical Beijing hutong presents an attractive indoor space through the world's most transparent window glass, donated by the same manufacturer who supplies Apple Store.

below: Layers of cut-out OSB engineered wood screens with shadow puppet patterns form a dramatic theatre space that is visually doubled in size by a full-wall mirror.

The 'Little Ants' also utilise their theatre space as a shop and classroom for additional income, and it attracts afterschool children from the nearby primary school.

Case Three: Letting 'Informal Density' Amalgamate

Since 2015, URBANUS has endeavoured to introduce 'informal density' into homogeneous courtyards with multiple households. By mixing workspaces for craftsmen with a residential complex, the gated courtyards will be open to the public.

A row of houses within a big hutong courtyard was chosen as an attractive site, as it looked like a narrow alley inside the complex. This site had a friendly and agreeable scale that was fitting for a craftsman community. Thus, it sparked the idea of creating a 'Home for the Craftsmen' by converting the row of houses into workshops in the front and an exhibition and lecture space in the back. To encourage residents to readily accept and welcome the craftsmen, URBANUS designed a double-door device to include different interactive space typologies for exchanges between the craftsmen and their neighbours. By manipulating open-and-closed modes of these two sets of doors, different types of interfaces can be determined for a variety of activities. For instance, when the first door is open to the alley, a small public niche is formed, while the opened glazed doors could be locked to the side walls to form a display window for artworks. This mode is particularly useful outside working hours, when the indoor space is unused while the narrow alley space needs to be amplified for the residents. Thus, the space between the two doors is temporarily lent to the neighbours, who can pull out a sliding table from the second door and flip down a chair on the first door to play chess or have a cup of tea. Here, architectural design plays the role of creating a community.

URBANUS,
Home for the Craftsmen,
Dashilar,
Beijing,
2015

The space of the narrow hutong alley is enlarged by the open workshop fronts which express a welcoming gesture from the shop owners to their neighbours.

'Informal Density' as a Tactical Strategy

Through successive ventures over these few years, URBANUS has realised that the implementation of 'informal density' in a region requires the formulation of a systematic strategy. The advantage of today's Chinese architects lies in the fact that they are not only involved in conventional architectural design, but also engaged in the design of society. This social-problem-solving position definitely requires pragmatic tactics. In the case of informal density, first of all, this type of density should take centre stage against the mainstream density. For example, the designs for Mr Zhang and the 'Little Ants' have earned curiosity and enthusiasm from their neighbours, who are willing to embrace the newcomers as new icons of their neighbourhoods. Secondly, careful design can help to connect 'informal density' with 'formal density' seamlessly. For example, the design of the double-door system in the 'Home for the Craftsmen' testifies that design can play a significant role in facilitating this connection. Thirdly, it must be realised that subjective good intentions do not necessarily result in successful realisation. For example, the construction of the 'Home for the Craftsmen' is still being blocked by some neighbours because they do not want to open up their private courtyard. Even worse, the recent political situation of expelling small businesses from the capital, Beijing, has stalled the project indefinitely.

Of course, the difficulties did not shake URBANUS's belief that making neighbourhood life more interesting is crucial in revitalising old urban areas. Therefore, a combination of re-anchoring craftsmen back into the old neighbourhoods, employing their crafts to energise the vitality of the community, and utilising their presence to shape distinctive characteristics of the community, forms an effective strategy. Parallel to URBANUS's interest in this issue, many other architects are also making similar efforts to gradually implant 'informal density' into 'formal density' to achieve an organic revitalisation for the old city. This collective consensus positions URBANUS at the dawn of urban renewal. ᴀ

The facade design for the 'Home for the Craftsmen' is a social device that uses a double-door system to encourage a friendly relationship between the existing local residents and the craftsman brought in through the 'informal density' project.

The back doors of the workshops are connected by a shared exhibition space whose display cases are designed as cabinets, where its old doors are collected from the demolition site as a reminiscence of the old hutong.

A New Protocol for Space Production

Generating Socially Cohesive Urban Architecture

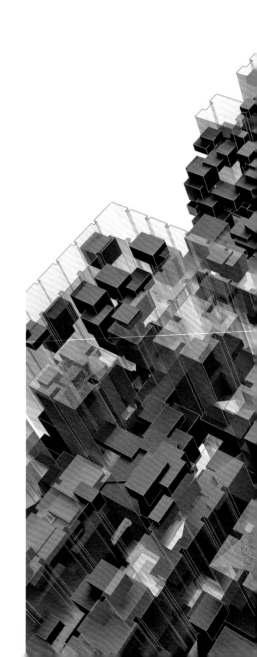

Shuo Wang

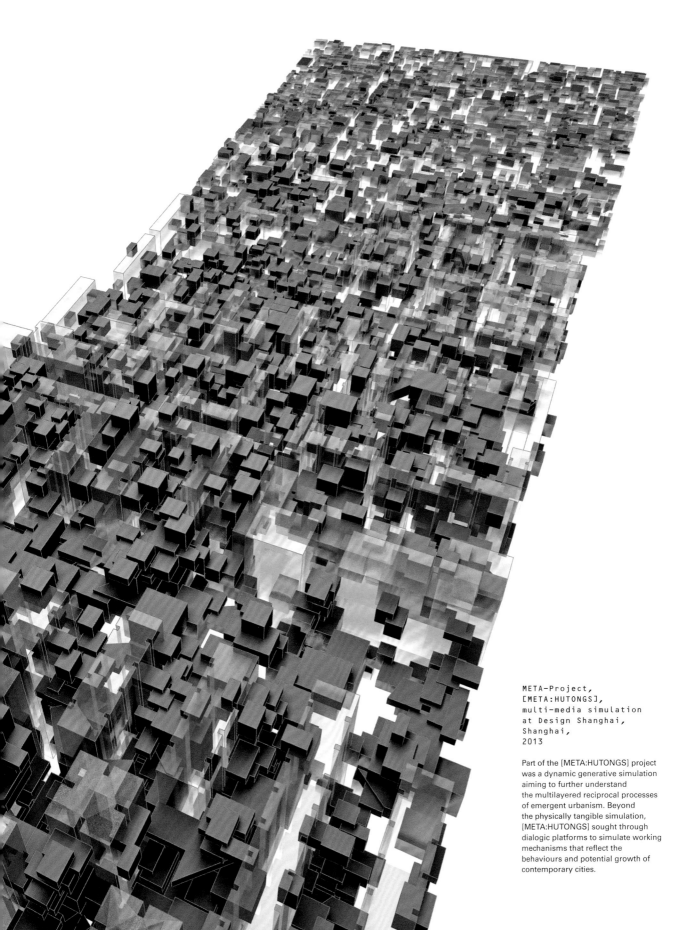

META-Project,
[META:HUTONGS],
multi-media simulation
at Design Shanghai,
Shanghai,
2013

Part of the [META:HUTONGS] project
was a dynamic generative simulation
aiming to further understand
the multilayered reciprocal processes
of emergent urbanism. Beyond
the physically tangible simulation,
[META:HUTONGS] sought through
dialogic platforms to simulate working
mechanisms that reflect the
behaviours and potential growth of
contemporary cities.

META-Project is a Beijing-based practice intent on improving quality of life in cities. Through a parallel research platform and an intermediate prototyping thread, it is exploring ways of using architecture to connect people to their social environment and promote positive interaction. Founding principal **Shuo Wang** outlines the evolution of META-Project's approach and documents several of its recent community-enhancing projects and investigations.

Our increasingly urbanised world presents new challenges and new opportunities. In the last two decades, contemporary urban developments have deviated from what was originally regarded as the paradigm of the 'modern city'. In particular, East Asian megacities such as Beijing, Shanghai, Hong Kong and Tokyo have been growing and changing at a mind-boggling speed.

Articles upon articles have described how factors including internet-based commerce, improved logistics, transnational flows of goods and the expansion of service industries on a global scale have all contributed to an extraordinary amount of growth in urban areas. To this day, cities' 'production of space'[1] has far surpassed the scope that the current discourse is able to describe. A new understanding of the city needs to be acquired from the current reality.

The city of Beijing presents a prime example of an emergent urban situation that has witnessed the wildest and most extreme changes. In the late 1990s, urban transformation started to erupt from overlapping layers of social, cultural, economic and everyday-life interrelations. The city has constantly reinvented itself based on ever-changing visions.

META-Project was founded in Beijing in 2009, with the intention of examining what is so enchanting about wild spaces in the contemporary reality, and bringing them back to stiffly planned city life. Parallel to the practice is META-Research, a contemporary urban culture platform that focuses on in-depth cross-disciplinary research on China's emergent urbanism.

Research as Knowledge Production

In 2012, META-Project initiated [META:HUTONGS], which became an award-winning and internationally renowned collaborative research venture. Grant-aided by the Graham Foundation and sponsored by the Urban China Initiative (UCI), the project investigated hutongs (narrow alleyways in the old core of Beijing) as laboratories that exemplify the current reality of Beijing's urban situation, and as key to potential urban regenerative strategies in the future. The aim was to build up an alternative mode of research that observes the contemporary reality from the point of view of one on the ground. Over a three-year period, it generated a network of knowledge production via workshops, symposiums, roundtable discussions and exhibitions. While creating new understanding to reveal the spatial-social quality of the unique urban emergence, the goal was to provide alternative approaches in order to instigate future projective possibilities.

[META:HUTONGS]'s outcomes have been well documented and broadcast extensively to a mass audience through print media, videos and a wiki-type website. Multimedia installations were exhibited in numerous events including Beijing Design Week, Design Shanghai, the Shenzhen & Hong Kong Bi-City Biennale of Urbanism\Architecture, and the Venice Biennale.

This new perspective on Beijing's contemporary urban reality also gave rise to heated discussions among the younger generation of architects, and led to the exhibition 'Building Issues' – co-curated by META-Project and Taikang Space, one of Beijing's high-profile contemporary art venues – showcasing eight young architects' urban research projects. The exhibition, which ran from 28 October to 9 December 2017, was well received by the public and earned the award for Best Social Observation Exhibition of the Year from China's *Art Trade Journal (Yi shu shang ye)*. Through this new engaging approach, 'research' has become a vehicle for the production and distribution of new knowledge about the city.

META-Project,
META-Project's working space,
Beijing,
2016

above: The office's premises feature islands of assembled modular furniture, developed as a prototype for flexible co-working space.

META-Project, [META:HUTONGS],
multi-media installation
at the 14th Venice Architecture
Biennale, Venice,
Italy,
2014

right: The installation presented [META:HUTONGS] as a process-based investigation of hutongs as a laboratory for knowledge production. The spatial relationship between physical models, images, text and video not only re-created a tangible sociocultural 'cross-section' of hutong spaces, but also became a key strategy to emulate complex urban phenomena.

Diagram showing the evolution of the shared-living prototype, developed from previous urban research across Chinese cities, and further iterated during the design process of the New Youth Commune project.

STANDARD ROOM MODEL

NEW NEIGHBOURHOOD MODEL

"THE TUBE" COLLECTIVE RESIDENCE TYPOLOGY

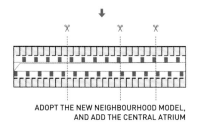

ADOPT THE NEW NEIGHBOURHOOD MODEL, AND ADD THE CENTRAL ATRIUM

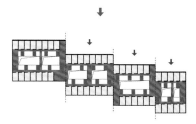

CUT 1 TO 4, RECONSTRUCT PUBLIC CIRCULATION THROUGH PASSAGE, BRIDGE AND OPEN CORNER SPACE

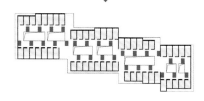

EXPAND OUTDOOR TERRACE FROM OPEN CORNER SPACE

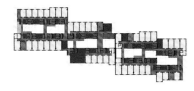

3rd FLOOR

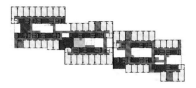

2nd FLOOR

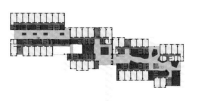

1st FLOOR

◁ ROOM   ■ W.C.   ▨ OUTDOOR PUBLIC SPACE   ▨ OPEN SPACE   ■ PUBLIC CIRCULATION   ■ NEIGHBOURHOOD SHARING SPACE

The shifting volume of the building seen from the main road, showing the south and east facade with multiple semi-public balconies – some shared by several neighbours, others connected with public programme. For example, at the front corner is a shared kitchen/dining space with independent entrance from ground level.

From Research to Prototype

What interests META-Project is how to decode the 'urban wildlife' gene and to gain knowledge that helps to improve urban inhabitants' lives. The practice is fully aware that there are many underlying contradictions, the reconciliation of which may not lie in the architectural domain. Therefore, architects need to dive into the grounded reality, to document, to reveal, to simulate, to envision and to debate, all with the goal of providing new ideas and methods for inducing effective interventions. Real strategies require not only a better understanding, but also a different protocol before applying it to practice: 'prototyping'. In 2015, 'META-Prototype' was introduced as an intermediate thread – an exploration to connect research to design. Since then, META-Project's new protocol has been based on a four-step process: (1) in-depth research of the reality; (2) further teasing out the knowledge produced from contemporary spaces, and integrating it with real users' demands; (3) developing the knowledge production into prototypes; and (4) applying the effective prototypes into practice.

One of the main focuses of META-Project's research is on the increasingly urgent issue of the younger generation living and working in the metropolis, and attempts to bring forward new prototypes of community that could work synergistically at multiple levels of social, cultural, economic and communal contexts.

Fuelled by the outcomes of the research, the New Youth Commune was one of the first prototypical projects that were realised. Based on sustained investigation of different emergent mixed-dwelling phenomena in China – from hutongs to villages-in-the-city to the so-called 'ant tribe' problems of young urban migrants – META-Project has accumulated knowledge on the underlying dynamics of such lived space[2] in the hybrid reality, which recognises a nuanced public–private spatial gradient in accordance with the unfolding relationship between everyday life and the neighbourhood. A new spatial prototype was proposed for restructuring communal space, which redefines 'shared living' in a flexible, plural and socio-ecological way. Soon after the residents moved in, a constant 'flow of everydayness' emerged in the communal spaces all over the building. The collective improvisations were not under the control of the 'designing', but were anticipated within the 'prototyping'.

Interior facade, looking across the atrium. A constant 'flow of everydayness' emerges in the communal spaces all over the building.

Initial programme distribution
diagram of the [Yan-Jing-Lane]
urban regeneration project,
which consists of co-living, co-
working and shared event spaces
in a semi-enclosed courtyard.

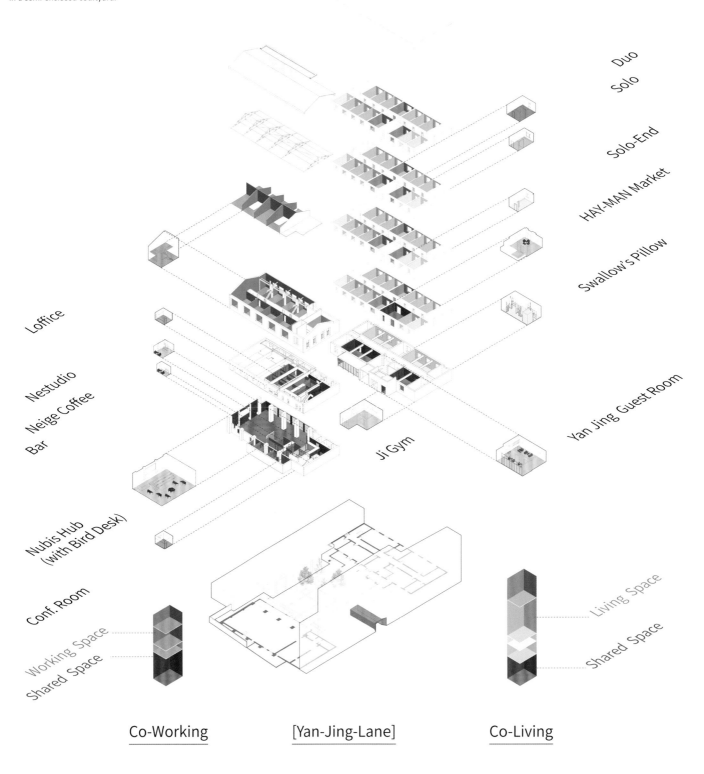

Duo

Solo

Solo-End

HAY-MAN Market

Swallow's Pillow

Loffice

Nestudio

Neige Coffee

Bar

Yan Jing Guest Room

Ji Gym

Nubis Hub
(with Bird Desk)

Conf. Room

Working Space

Shared Space

Living Space

Shared Space

Co-Working

[Yan-Jing-Lane]

Co-Living

Optimising the Protocol

While the results of this new protocol of 'research–prototype–practice' are remarkably inspiring, it is also recognised that only through continually iterating and improving can a prototype be developed into effective practice. Therefore, a building's completion must not be the end point. Starting with the New Youth Commune, META-Project has been positively trying to engage more with the underlying mechanisms that form a community. The recent project [Yan-Jing-Lane] became a perfect base for experiment.

[Yan-Jing-Lane] is a 2017 urban regeneration project that consists of co-living, co-working and shared event spaces in a semi-open introverted courtyard, forming a hybrid and self-driven community. To further push the exploration of the protocol for spatial production, META-Project became a partner in the core development/operation team. It not only kept injecting a plural cultural programme into the community protocols, but also took the role of readjusting both the hardware (architectural intervention) and the software (operational mechanism) through a series of post-occupancy evaluations, especially on everyday interpersonal interactions.

Eventually, the question may concern how to transcend the hybridity of China's contemporary reality, and to propose a new paradigm of social cohesiveness that promotes mutual collaboration and positive interaction. META-Project believes that it is the task of this generation's Chinese architects to further explore this and find a solution. In this light, architecture is no longer merely physical spaces made with constituent elements of structure, material, light etc; instead it turns multi-dimensional in making connections between people and their social environment. Thus, architecture becomes not just a 'protocol of design', but a 'protocol of knowledge'.[3]

What Defines META-Project's Approach

META-Project believes that in the face of today's new challenges, architecture needs to evolve from a situation obscured by the accumulation of 'things',[4] to a new level of clarity and complexity. The answer lies in seeking out a new protocol for integrating research, prototype and design practice within the overall cycle of the production of space.

META-Project's explorations aim to establish a new relationship between architecture and its social environment, so as to show a new reality where architecture is not just a frozen reflection of our society, nor a naive expression of an unsustainable utopia, but effective intervention to promote new values of contemporary life. ᴆ

Notes
1. Henri Lefebvre, 'From Absolute Space to Abstract Space', in *The Production of Space*, Wiley-Blackwell (Cambridge), 1992, p 246.
2. Edward Soja, 'The Trialectics of Spatiality', in *Thirdspace: Journeys to Los Angeles and Other Real-and-Imagined Places*, Blackwell (Oxford), 1996, pp 53–82.
3. Mark Jarzombek, 'A Conceptual Introduction to Architecture', *Log*, 15, Anyone Corporation (New York City), 2009, pp 89–98.
4. Kazimir Malevich, 'Suprematism', in *The Non-Objective World: The Manifesto of Suprematism*, Dover Publications (Mineola, NY), 2003, p 74.

Nubis Hub – a flexible event space in [Yan-Jing-Lane] which can be switched between co-working/lecture hall/party/ballroom modes at different time slots, according to users' requests.

Three Main Drivers of Sustainable Design

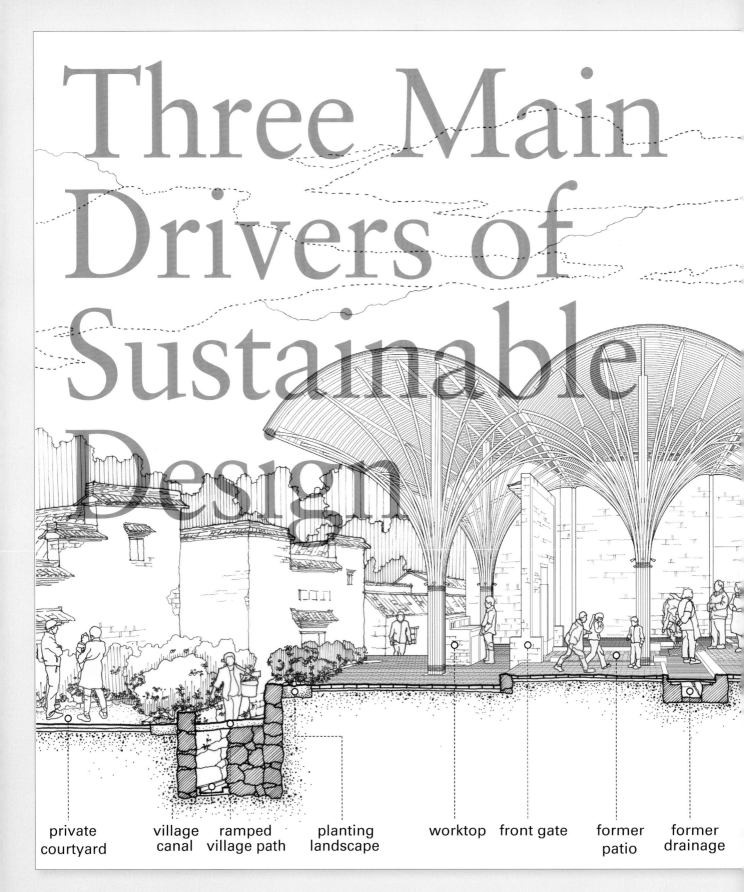

private courtyard · village canal · ramped village path · planting landscape · worktop · front gate · former patio · former drainage

SUP Atelier is a practice that experiments with advanced sustainable design. Their projects are notable for how they integrate local materials and traditional craftsmanship into total environmental solutions. The office's architect in chief **Yehao Song**, who also directs the Institute for Architecture and Technology at Beijing's Tsinghua University, presents some of their recent work, focusing around the three essential aims that drive their approach.

A New Architectural Vernacular for China

Yehao Song

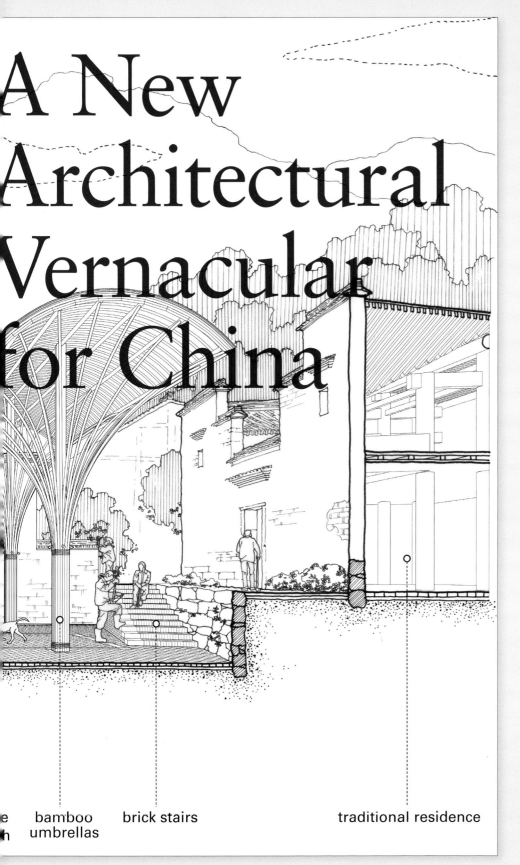

bamboo
umbrellas

brick stairs

traditional residence

Yehao Song / SUP Atelier,
Village Lounge,
Shangcun,
Jixi county,
Anhui province,
2017

Section perspective with construction
details of bamboo structures and
renovation of traditional courtyard.

In contemporary China, there is a significant imbalance in rates of development between the eastern coastal provinces and the western inner country, and between cities and rural areas. Grounded in the search for a sustainable design strategy that is suitable and localised for the various parts of the country, Song und Partner Atelier (SUP Atelier) has developed three focus points through practice: the use of natural resources; the embodiment of cultural diversity; and the adoption of suitable technologies.

Using Natural Resources

The use of natural resources in buildings – in terms of both energy and materials – has always been important within China's age-old architectural tradition, and is also a key part of sustainable design in the country today. Under the premise of satisfying bioclimatic comfort needs in different climate zones and among different groups of people through architectural design, solar energy and natural ventilation are widely utilised to reduce the consumption of non-renewable energy, and sustainable natural materials are employed to reduce the use of artificial materials. For example, in China, the use of solar energy generally involves two measures: photovoltaic panels and solar collectors. The presence of the two types of additional equipment influences buildings' appearance. Similarly, natural ventilation has long been an important measure for the Chinese in regulating the impact of climate. The two fundamental driving forces of natural air circulation – buoyance and wind pressure – are both directly related to architecture. Buoyance is commonly attained in architectural design by means of either a tall wind tower that encourages air circulation through a chimney effect, or a Venturi tube in the section of the building. Wind pressure can be created by adding architectural elements that resemble spoilers. Energy savings and regulation of climate comfort can be achieved to a higher degree through the implementation of both buoyance and wind pressure methods.

The Tsinghua Eco Studio (THE Studio) in Gui'an, Guizhou province, completed in 2015, exemplifies SUP Atelier's approach to using natural resources. Regarding the layout, it is a long, tall exhibition hall with relatively closed functional rooms to either side. Long, narrow skylights not only enhance natural ventilation through the chimney effect, but also provide the space with natural light. Moreover, the coloured thin-film photovoltaic glass adds liveliness to the atrium's atmosphere. Coloured rays are projected through the glass and the wooden trusses onto the interior walls and floors, and the light and shade changes with the seasons and times of day. Regarding the materials, a large number of renewable ones such as wood, steel, and straw panels are used, and the adoption of unique native materials and processes is encouraged: for example, the traditional rattan weave process is applied to the facade system, *qingshi* (bluestone) is used for the interior floors, and rubble masonry is used for the external enclosure. All of these can effectively reduce the building's carbon footprint throughout the building's life cycle and meanwhile create a unique architectural expression.

Also completed by SUP Atelier in 2015 was the Central Canteen of Tsinghua University, Beijing, which houses not only a canteen for students and staff, but also a careers centre for graduates. A corridor running from east to west across the building separates the canteen from the careers centre. Seven oval-shaped skylights in the corridor bring natural air circulation through hot air pressure and wind pressure ventilation to the three-storey atrium in the warm months via openings designed on the side of each skylight. Abundant natural light and efficient energy savings are achieved alongside an effective cooling strategy in the summer.

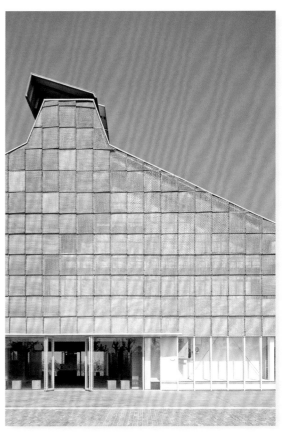

The west elevation, with its vernacular double-skin facade system using rattan – a natural, climate-friendly material that also engages with local craft traditions.

Yehao Song / SUP Atelier,
Tsinghua Eco Studio (THE Studio),
Gui'an,
Guizhou province,
2015

The central atrium – a multifunctional entrance hall for exhibitions and conferences. The structure is in timber, with a raised roof for natural lighting and ventilation.

View from the southwest, with
surrounding landscaping.
The building serves as both a
canteen and a careers centre.

Yehao Song / SUP Atelier,
Central Canteen of Tsinghua University,
Beijing,
2015

The three-storey atrium benefits
from plenty of natural light and
natural ventilation.

*Abundant natural
light and efficient
energy savings are
achieved alongside
an effective
cooling strategy
in the summer.*

The southeast corner features a café terrace
with retained original sycamore trees
and a brick masonry handcraft artwork wall.

The configuration of the bamboo umbrella and the arch of the black awning are similar in scale to the traditional black-tiled roofs, blending into the fabric of the village.

Yehao Song / SUP Atelier,
Village Lounge,
Shangcun,
Jixi county,
Anhui province,
2017

Aerial view of the village of Shangcun,
with the new Village Lounge at its
heart to accommodate villagers' and
visitors' activities.

Under the roof of bamboo, the
Village Lounge sits within a
courtyard, and features a reinforced
section of traditional brick wall.

Embodying Cultural Diversity

Finding the most suitable materials, construction methods and usage patterns for the spirit of Chinese building, and contributing design power to the preservation of cultural diversity, are indispensable and important parts of sustainable design.

SUP Atelier's project for a Village Lounge in Shangcun, Jixi county, Anhui province, completed in 2017, collected and organised old black bricks, black tiles, stones and usable timbers from the site to form landscape elements based on the original layout of the courtyard. The design solution was grounded on the principle of minimal intervention, adopting a plan of multiple units using a common local material – bamboo – to construct six large sheltered spaces. The six 5-by-5-metre (16-by-16-foot) spaces form three sets of bamboo canopies with black awnings, providing a shared space to host the activities of village locals and visitors. The configuration of the bamboo umbrella and the arch of the black awning are similar in scale to the traditional black-tiled roofs, blending into the fabric of the village.

At THE Studio in Gui'an, the climate-responsive double-skin facade system applies a local handicraft product: woven rattan. Although the outer layer of the skin, which consists of four densities of rattan units, is based on the results of simulations of solar radiation and wind pressure distribution on the building's surface, the rattan comes from local craftsmen, supporting the development of the ancient local rattan heritage. On the ground floor, an open and fluid route is designed to provide same-level entrances to different interfaces spatially, creating a communicative public space for students and staff who are coming from different parts of the campus. Landscaping outside the building continues the original site formation with respect to the existing plantation. The building sets back on the southeast corner in order to retain a historic Chinese parasol tree. The thoughtful approach to the history of the site helps to initiate a dynamic modern campus life.

Adopting Suitable Technologies

In China's urban centres, sustainable designs primarily need to reflect high technical content, high budgets and high operational and maintenance standards, as well as having a level of bioclimatic comfort that is consistent with international standards. In rural areas, the need is more for low-cost projects with low technical specifications. Exemplifying a third type of project that represents the vast quantity of construction in contemporary China is the Central Canteen of Tsinghua University. Like its surrounding buildings, it takes brick, characterised by its low cost and high artistic value, as its material. With various forms of masonry, the bricks form rich and varied interfaces, matching the different scenes of the campus. Through the structural design of the skylights and brick walls, and the common construction techniques and raw materials, the building achieves a high degree of comfort and interest, while reducing operational and maintenance costs. ∆

Xiao Fu and Wei You

Basic Green Building Design

Reconnecting Sustainability to the Vernacular

Integrated Architecture Studio,
Huilongshan Kindergarten,
Changxing county,
Zhejiang province,
2017

The northwest corner of the two-storey box called 'the Fun Cube' is partially lowered to one storey to let in sunshine. This shape manipulation provides the possibility of lighting and ventilation for the large and deep square box, and becomes the key factor in the creation of spatial quality.

Given cultural differences in lifestyles and building usage, Western techniques for measuring sustainability are ill fitted to the Chinese context. Instead of relying on international certification systems like LEED, China needs a homegrown solution to improve its green building credentials. The Integrated Architecture Studio at Nanjing University has established such a methodology, combining sustainable design with spatial and tectonic pursuits to achieve integrated architectural quality. **Xiao Fu**, the studio's leader, and his colleague and research collaborator **Wei You**, explain its motivations and illustrate some of its outcomes.

Ever since the 1980s, Chinese architects have regarded Western contemporary architecture as their reference point. Rather than engaging with the vernacular, they have been focusing on whether their works fulfil Western technical standards and aesthetics. The same applies to the development of sustainable architecture. To a large degree, before 2006, green building in China equalled the LEED certification in the US. In 2006, China established the National Evaluation Standard for Green Building with reference to Western standards. Despite this, few of the country's architects actively use green elements during the creative process; instead, they have technicians carry out the indicator calculations after the design is completed. So, does the future of Chinese green building lie merely in Western technical standards? Is 'green building' limited to the sense of criteria and indicators?

Since 2010, the members of the Integrated Architecture Studio (IA) at Nanjing University have been reflecting and experimenting on this issue based on a 'vernacular problem'-oriented approach. They have put forward the notion of 'Basic Green Building Design', which aims for the return of green elements to design and the vernacular lifestyle. Through a series of projects, they have explored the development of a green building design approach that is suitable for contemporary China.

Bringing Sustainability Back to Vernacular Issues

In China, other than in especially cold regions, common buildings such as schools, offices and residential blocks are not fully equipped with climate-control systems. Halls, corridors, stairways, bathrooms and other public spaces rely entirely on natural climate control; only the rooms where people spend longer periods of time are exceptions. Even in these rooms, people generally minimise the use of equipment in order to keep costs down – through putting on or taking off clothes, standing up and moving around, opening windows to let air in, or limited use of lighting. For example, in the House of Reduced Air Conditioning Use, Nanjing (2011), designed by IA, the client demanded that the house should use passive design to reduce the use of air conditioning as much as possible. Moreover, although many public buildings in China are equipped with mechanical ventilation systems, these systems are seldom turned on. In contrast, buildings in some Western countries are fully equipped with control systems, and the total operation time of these systems per year is way longer than that of Chinese buildings. The Chinese style of building usage, then, is considerably different from that of the West, at least concerning energy consumption, so we cannot refer completely to Western architecture. Where does the direction of Chinese green building design lie? This question has recently caught the attention of some Chinese scholars, and even key national research and development programmes have started to fund related studies. According to the status quo in China, IA believes that 'green' should be treated as a basic design approach, to return to the actual lifestyle of the Chinese people, and to improve architectural quality.

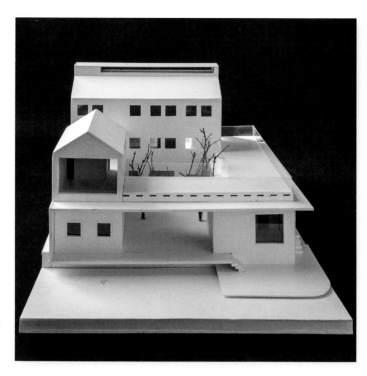

Model. The client wanted to maintain room temperature at around 30 degrees Celsius (86 degrees Fahrenheit) in the hottest months and around 15 Celsius (60 Fahrenheit) in the coldest months through passive climate control measures, so as to reduce the use of air conditioning as much as possible.

Integrated Architecture Studio,
House of Reduced Air Conditioning Use,
Nanjing,
2011

IA believes that 'green' should be treated as a basic design approach, to return to the actual lifestyle of the Chinese people, and to improve architectural quality.

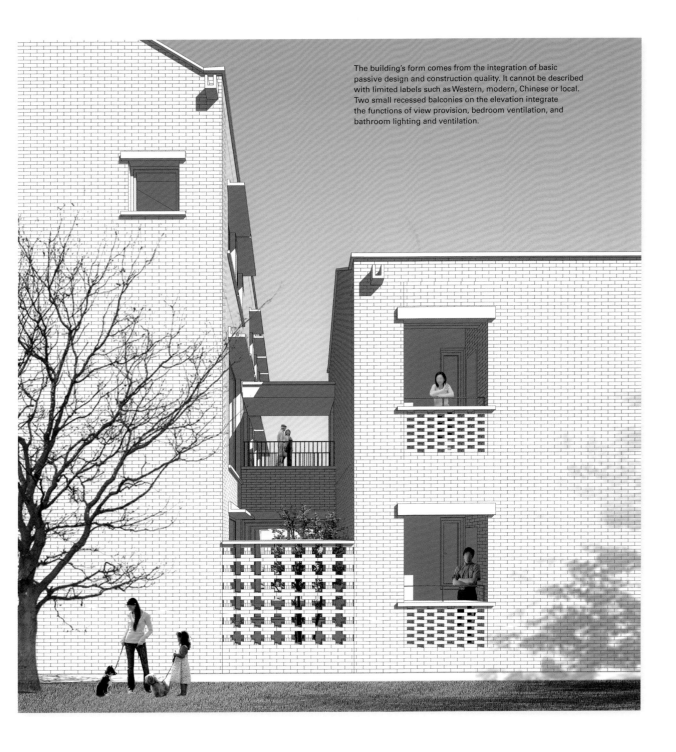

The building's form comes from the integration of basic passive design and construction quality. It cannot be described with limited labels such as Western, modern, Chinese or local. Two small recessed balconies on the elevation integrate the functions of view provision, bedroom ventilation, and bathroom lighting and ventilation.

Computer simulation. At lower right is a wind environment simulation, determining the relationship between the building layout, the courtyard opening and the wind direction. At upper right is an analysis of the temperature fluctuations in each room under different passive climate control designs.

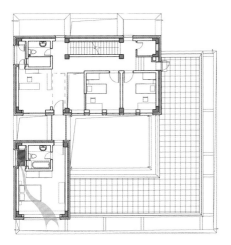

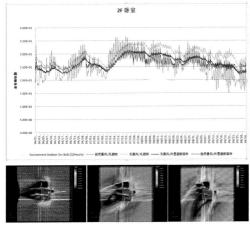

Firstly, sustainability is more about design than about indicator statistics. Basic Green Building Design aims to integrate green elements into the design of architectural space and form, and emphasises the active effects of green elements during the stage of conceptual design. It also pays attention to architectural quality, because when green buildings lack design quality, they become lifeless. Basic Green Building Design emphasises using computers to simulate performance, in order to make up for the shortage in design experience. Nevertheless, IA objects to the excess of technological rationalities, and aims to pursue the 'better' rather than the 'best': pursuing the 'best' may result in buildings as mere machinery without humanity, thus lacking the sustainability of cultural ecology.

Secondly, the use of green elements should return to the vernacular lifestyle to respond to the Chinese model of energy consumption. Basic Green Building Design emphasises the use of passive green elements that have been devised in response to the natural climate and according to the actual lifestyle of Chinese people, including natural lighting, natural ventilation, heat preservation, insulation and sun shading. It is worth mentioning that Western buildings which are fully equipped with control systems also pay attention to the value of passive design, so as to reduce the equipment's energy consumption while ensuring comfort. Under the Chinese model of energy consumption, the contents of passive design are more diversified. In unequipped spaces, the significance of passive design lies in direct climate control and improvement of comfort; in equipped spaces, passive design still functions towards direct climate control and the improvement of comfort, due to Chinese people's thrifty habits of equipment usage. In contrast with the Western model, which achieves accurate degrees of comfort through equipment with high energy consumption levels, the Chinese model achieves more inaccurate degrees of comfort but with low energy consumption, through the climate's adjustment and people's behaviour. The two models are different in the philosophical sense, with the Western model adjusting the environment to humans, and the Chinese model, the very reverse.

Practices of Basic Green Building Design

In recent years, IA has been adopting the Basic Green Building Design approach in a series of projects. With the office building of Nanjing Zidong International Service Centre (2011), the studio combined rooftop photovoltaic solar energy utilisation with an improvement of the spatial qualities of the interior. In the Xiqiao Canteen project for the 2014 Qingdao International Horticultural Exposition, IA used thermal analysis of solar radiation to maximise views of the surrounding landscape from the dining space. And with the Huilongshan Kindergarten in Changxing county, Zhejiang province (2017), IA profoundly explored the Basic Green Building Design approach under the Chinese model of energy consumption.

Integrated Architecture Studio,
Xiqiao Canteen,
2014 Qingdao International
Horticultural Exposition,
Qingdao, Shandong province,
2014

Based on computer simulations of solar radiation, the design gives the dining space the greatest possible amount of glass wall for viewing the landscape.

In the Xiqiao Canteen project for the 2014 Qingdao International Horticultural Exposition, IA used thermal analysis of solar radiation to maximise views of the surrounding landscape from the dining space.

The pitched roof not only provides a
suitable angle for the installation of rooftop
photovoltaic panels, but also increased space
height for the exhibition hall. The suspended
multimedia hall takes full advantage of the
increased space height while not hindering
spatial fluidity.

Integrated Architecture Studio,
Huilongshan Kindergarten,
Changxing county,
Zhejiang province,
2017

Passive shape manipulations were adopted in response to the climate and orientation, including two windows on a diagonal line, an upward-pitched roof and two staggered skylights.

The 3-metre (10-foot) overhanging eave at the main entrance forms a horizontal southeast shade, while offering a semi-outdoor space with the wooden platform as the children's playground and the parents' waiting area.

Two staggered skylights are placed at the spot with the least lighting and ventilation, and the position and size of the atrium skylight are determined through computer simulation. Children playing on the roof can 'peep' into the atrium through the skylights.

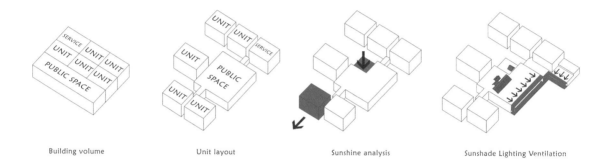

Building volume

Unit layout

Sunshine analysis

Sunshade Lighting Ventilation

The two opposing corner windows solved the lighting and ventilation issues of the deep space inside the cubes. They also increased communications between various rooms. Children can see other children while playing, which prevents them from feeling lonely.

ANSYS® Airpak® and DAYSIM software were used to optimise the ventilation and lighting. Lifting up the roof significantly improved the multifunctional room's lighting and increased its ventilation rate from twice to four times per hour, bringing away redundant heat and helping to prevent disease proliferation in the densely populated space.

In this project, because of the limited size of the site, several public activity rooms are gathered into a square 'box' called 'the Fun Cube'. The compact layout allows more outdoor activity spaces to be made available. Passive shape manipulations were adopted in response to the climate and orientation, including two windows on a diagonal line, an upward-pitched roof and two staggered skylights, to solve the lighting and ventilation problem and meanwhile improve the spatial quality. For example, the pitched roof creates space for the children's gallery and a grandstand while improving the lighting and ventilation of the multi-function room; the two windows on the diagonal line ensure the lighting in the deepest part of the Cube (the hall), and also strengthen the permeation and connection among spaces. These shape manipulations can only be done during the conceptual stage; they are comprehensive deductive results based on the integration of previous design experiences, computer performance simulation and spatial quality.

Surpassing the Basic

Basic Green Building Design is an approach aimed at resolving the misunderstanding of fundamental green building issues in contemporary China, rather than a brand-new notion. When green elements really return in design, and become one of our sources for creating architectural quality, it will be more than 'basic'; it will surpass basic, becoming an effective approach and method for Chinese architects to respond to the vernacular lifestyle. This is only the beginning. ⌂

The pitched roof not only optimises the lighting and ventilation of the multifunction activity room, but also creates space for the children's gallery and the roof grandstand. When the interior space needs ventilation, the administrator can manually open the window on the roof activity platform.

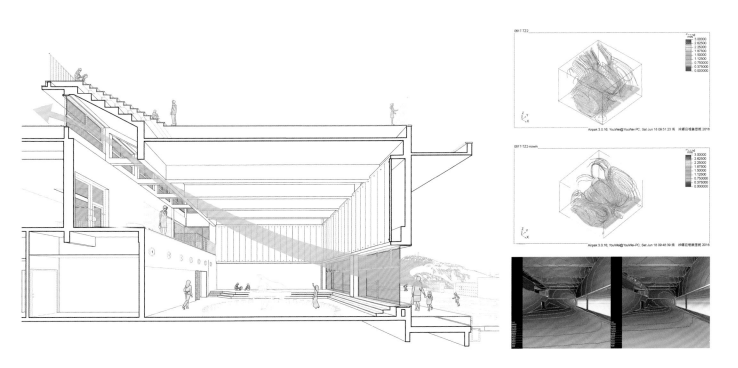

Text © 2018 John Wiley & Sons Ltd. Images: pp 80-1, 86(t&b), 87(t) © Bowen Hou; pp 82-3, 86(c), 87(b) © Xiao Fu; pp 84-5 © Yao Li

Yichun Liu

Responsive Structure

Architecture as a Thing-scape

Atelier Deshaus,
Café and souvenir shop
of the Modern Art Museum,
Pudong,
Shanghai,
2016

Exploded axonometric. Abandonment
gradually turns architecture transparent
through weathering. The coexistence
of old and new structures is a different
type of premeditated transparency.

Structure should be not just a technical issue, but integral to architectural expression. As architect **Yichun Liu** argues here, the modern separation of architecture from structural engineering in both education and professional practice is impoverishing the built environment. The office that he co-founded, Atelier Deshaus, has evolved a new model of design that involves close collaboration with engineers from the outset, to generate works that respond richly to their physical and cultural context. Four projects in Shanghai, where the firm is based, illustrate how it works.

Structure-related issues are fundamental in architecture. It is reflections on the currently distant working relationship between architects and engineers that have recently led the Shanghai practice Atelier Deshaus to revisit the importance of structure. The separation is apparent across the entire building industry in contemporary China. In Chinese architectural education, the subject of structure is independent from the subject of architecture, which aggravates the distance between the two even further in the professional capacity after graduation. At the same time, the dominance of political factors in the decision-making process for the construction of the country's public buildings has had the adverse effect of simplification and symbolisation in design. The more important the building is, the more prominent its symbolic features are. The winning design proposal is often chosen for the superficial reason of having features that are highly recognisable and iconic. The building's structure vanishes behind these features, its function retreating to merely a platform for the symbolism.

When preparing the design of the Long Museum West Bund in Shanghai in 2012, Atelier Deshaus consulted countless structural engineers. Confronted with the design challenge of such a cantilevered structure, most of them were resigned to the confines of the political system's requirements. Some considered that such a design could not be categorised into any established structural system; some, that it would never be able to pass the council's seismic assessment. Even though all of them agreed a vault-umbrella structure would be entirely suitable to bear the loads, they suggested the use of a standard steel frame with a skin designed to the architect's 'desire' – a much safer and more easily applied method. Later, the young structural engineer Zhun Zhang showed up and solved the so-called systematic and standardisation problem admirably and without too much difficulty. He applied small connecting lintels to differentiate the loadbearing system so that it would suit all levels of seismic impact. This design solution also extended the originally spatial vault-umbrella, which had grown from the frame structure that already existed on the site, to a vault-umbrella that is structural, achieving consistency and the space defined by such consistency, in accordance with Atelier Deshaus's original vision.

This article does not intend to discuss the process of achieving an anticipated form in architecture, or whether it is more commendable to achieve such form through structural or, rather, non-structural practices. What is important is the issue of structural engineering gradually being separated from an architect's work, as a result of both autonomous subjects in education and division of labour in the profession today. It is a common phenomenon, with modern architects no longer required to be generalists in both art and technology like their Renaissance counterparts; an operating model consists of overtly job-specified professionals. The requirement for collaboration has resulted in the loss of both the self-evident nature of structures and the ultimate simplicity achieved through rigorous thinking. This misplaced modernity is particularly evident in architectural practice in contemporary China.

Atelier Deshaus,
Long Museum West Bund,
Xuhui,
Shanghai,
2014

Shown here while under construction in 2013, the independent cantilever concrete vault-umbrella structure is spatial as well as functional.

Objectivity and the Thing-scape

The design of the Long Museum West Bund, completed in 2014, has led Atelier Deshaus to experience the energy that structural elements can generate in space. The Middle Hall of the Tianwang Temple in Changzi county, Shanxi province, constructed during the Jin dynasty (1115–1234 AD), is a case in point. It was in the summer of the same year that I paid a visit there and was struck by the gigantic timber columns and beams that almost fill the entire space. Instead of triggering any thoughts as to how they were constructed, however, what is more profound is the emotion provoked by the quality of the space, surprisingly similar to that generated in the Long Museum. The structural system of age-old Chinese architecture is based on experience, not on scientific calculations, but what we can still feel is the crucial part that structural elements played in creating and defining a space. They exist all around us, but at the same time disappear into the space they create. Such structure, responsive to both the physical and cultural context, embodies a state of objectivity in its own right. It is a state in which the functionality is no longer a dominant way of understanding structural elements; rich connotations of time, space, site etc are implied through their appearance. The scene hence created with these objects is what could be considered as a thing-scape. It is a desirable state, yet is almost impossible for architects to achieve alone, or even with structural engineers in the conventional working model.

Tianwang Temple, Changzi county, Shanxi province, Jin dynasty (1115–1234)

Gigantic timber columns and beams fill the space and determine its quality.

Objectivity originally meant having a matter-of-fact attitude towards life and objects. In so doing, it simultaneously requires a reflection and inquiry into the essence of things. The word can be easily connected to the late 19th-/early 20th-century German architectural theory of *Sachlichkeit*.[1] Architecture is a subject involved with and defined by many other subjects. Its ontology and autonomy are constantly evolving and debated. *Sachlichkeit* first appeared as a response to architectural realism, and was consequently applied in discussions of new facts faced by architecture and the rising imbalance between time, location, language and form. If structure can reappear with the backdrop of Chinese contemporary architecture, it can be understood as a contemporary action of *Sachlichkeit* and a belated modernity.

Working with Structural Engineers

Since the design of Long Museum West Bund, Atelier Deshaus has gradually formed a working mode that involves structural engineers in the whole process of architectural design. By means of constant communication and efforts to understand each other's role, a collaborative process is established to convert structure from merely a technical element to part of the vocabulary for spatial construction and architectural context.

The following three recent projects – the Blossom Pavilion, the teahouse in the Li Garden, and the café and souvenir shop of the Modern Art Museum, all in Shanghai – describe how this collaboration between architecture and structure is established. On the one hand, the architects introduce the structural engineers to the architectural design process by proposing questions such as 'How can we achieve the maximum cantilever of a single steel board with six supporting points?', 'How can we achieve a reasonable structure with equal-sized horizontal and vertical parts?', 'How slender can they be?', or 'How can we incorporate a secondary structural system into an existing structure?' In fact, structural questions such as these already have implied architectural intention, and they establish a path for structure to eventually make the leap away from being a mere technical element. On the other hand, these three small projects present three entirely different approaches to structural expression.

The Blossom Pavilion is a spatial installation designed in collaboration with artist Wang Zhan for the 2015 Shanghai Urban Space Art Season. Although it is a spatial interpretation of the artist's sculpture work *Artificial Rocks*, it began with a rigorous, even painstaking, structural design. The 12-by-8-metre (39-by-26-foot) cover consists of steel boards in two thicknesses – 8 and 14 millimetres (0.315 and 0.551 inch) – arranged in a grid according to the load they are bearing. Cloud-like ribbed slabs 14 millimetres (0.551 inch) thick and of various heights (50–200 millimetres (2–8 inches)) sit above the steel boards, whilst underneath, six 60-by-60-millimetre (2.36-by-2.36-inch) single or A-shaped solid square steel columns are arranged according to spatial requirements. These elements all bear loads, the size and position of which stem from careful decisions made by the architects along with the structural engineers. However, these precise, if not perfect, structural elements did not appear completely in the finished architecture. Specially treated stainless-steel facing made by the artist covered all of the carefully positioned columns, while the gradually rusted steel ceiling gained a sense of lightness thanks to the polished finish of its supports. The space is an abstracted rock garden that brings visitors a sense of bewilderment.

Wang Zhan, *Artificial Rock No 85*, 2005

The renowned Chinese modern sculptor Wang Zhan uses mirrored stainless steel to imitate rock formations in Chinese gardens. It is a departure from nature, but a connection with the modern city. It is also a representation of objectivity.

The architect resolved and transformed the *Artificial Rocks* into an abstract rock-like space, reinterpreting the pavilion as an architectural typology.

The space is a rock garden that fills visitors with bewilderment.

This structural axonometric drawing appears complete as an architectural type – the pavilion. It is a very precise and very minimal industrial construction in the style of Mies van der Rohe.

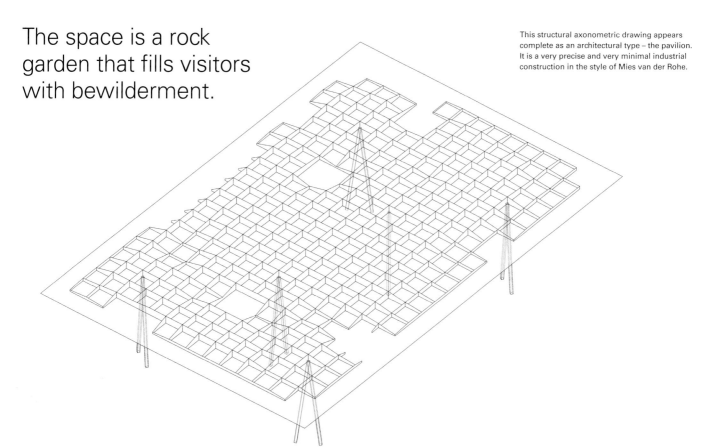

The artist deliberately chose stainless steel as the surface of the sides, which has a similar texture to stone rubbings. The surrounding plantation is blended into this pavilion through a blurred visual experience.

Atelier Deshaus,
Teahouse in Li Garden,
Xuhui,
Shanghai,
2016

A paulownia tree living very close by in the garden. Its trunk, 90 centimetres (35 inches) in circumference, became an important spatial element, bringing the small courtyard at the back into the interior of the teahouse.

The teahouse in the Li Garden was completed in 2016. The most important design intention of this piece lies within the questions presented to the structural engineer. By adopting the same measurements for all horizontal and vertical supporting units, it was hoped that these units could form an abstract visual composition, realising their potential beyond that of structural elements. With both a length and a width of 60 millimetres (2.362 inches), the units are at the same scale as furniture, and create a more intimate relationship between the building and the body. It is this intimacy that blends the space of the teahouse into the garden completely. To achieve a lightness for the structure situated within the garden, the architect asked the engineer to design a top-down frame, using the entrance door and the wall of the service area at the north side to support the roof, while at the same time cantilevering the beam on both ends to hang two different levels of horizontal boards. This would give a 'floating' effect in the courtyard with hanging corner columns; however, in doing so, the horizontal boards are inclined to sway when bearing people's weight. As a solution, the engineer extended the internal columns to the ground to become a loadbearing unit, forming a structure that balances the upper and lower parts. The internal columns support the horizontal boards from the ground, bearing the load upwards, whilst external columns bear the load of the boards downwards through suspension, and are off the ground. Different architectural units combine to create a flexible structural system that works on the balance between different forces. The physics between overhanging and suspension on the upper part allow the slender columns below to touch the ground gently, therefore achieving a close relationship where structural intention and architectural intention go hand in hand.

A three-layered slender cantilever structure reduces the footprint of the teahouse, giving more space back to the garden.

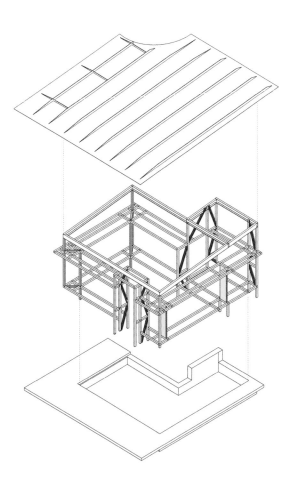

Diagram of the teahouse's structure. Black indicates loadbearing transferring columns; yellow, side boards of bookshelves; and red, lateral supporting units.

Atelier Deshaus,
Café and souvenir shop
of the Modern Art Museum,
Pudong,
Shanghai,
2016

The glass boxes with roofs suspended from the steel structure create a new time and scale system below the abandoned coal transport path.

Also completed in 2016, the café and souvenir shop of the Modern Art Museum, Shanghai, was converted from an abandoned coal-loading bridge. The design added a new steel frame and suspension system to the existing structure, supported by the ruin-like concrete frames left on the site. It not only strengthens the original structure, providing a secondary structure to the promenade above, but also functions as a suspension system for the glass café and the roof of the souvenir shop dotted beneath the elevated walkway. The glass cubes need no further vertical support, and are featured with transparent glass corners and fluid spaces. The standard and common glass spatial unit brought new life to this once abandoned and meaningless old dock, creating a new time and scale system, while merging into the surroundings, gentle, anonymous and easygoing. As user and viewer, we are able to choose between investigation or oblivion – a state that not only represents the structure's manner of existence within the setting, but also the modernity of Shanghai as a metropolis. The intervention of the new structure reinvented the old structure, without utilising its entire loadbearing potential. The integration and interaction of precisely calculated new structure and excessive old structure demonstrates a responsiveness to time.

Structure Can Be Emotional

These three projects are small structures in the mega urban space of Shanghai. Although they still appear to be discussing the practical issue of construction, they bring warmth to the cold industrial materials, and a sense of happiness that is small but certain. The continuous and evolving thoughts in these projects prove that structure can serve space, body and context in many different ways. Once structure is able to transform into a spatial and symbolic role from an element merely bearing loads, it has the ability to appear and disappear from our view, and to produce firm and powerful emotions. The perception called forth is about structure, time and location; it is fine, precise and never excessive. It is generated firstly in the intelligence, and transformed later into emotions. In this way, structure goes towards the scenery of things, or 'thing-scape'. ∆

Note
1. Otto Wagner, *Modern Architecture: A Guidebook for his Students to this Field of Art* (introduction and translation by Harry Francis Mallgrave), Getty Center for the History of Art and the Humanities (Los Angeles, CA), 1988. Mallgrave translates *Sachlichkeit* as 'Objectivity' in his English introduction.

The new steel structure, while clamping the old concrete column, also supports the upper structure. It hangs down from the steel truss, which rests on the old concrete-framed girder.

Once structure is able to transform into a spatial and symbolic role from an element merely bearing loads, it has the ability to appear and disappear from our view, and to produce firm and powerful emotions.

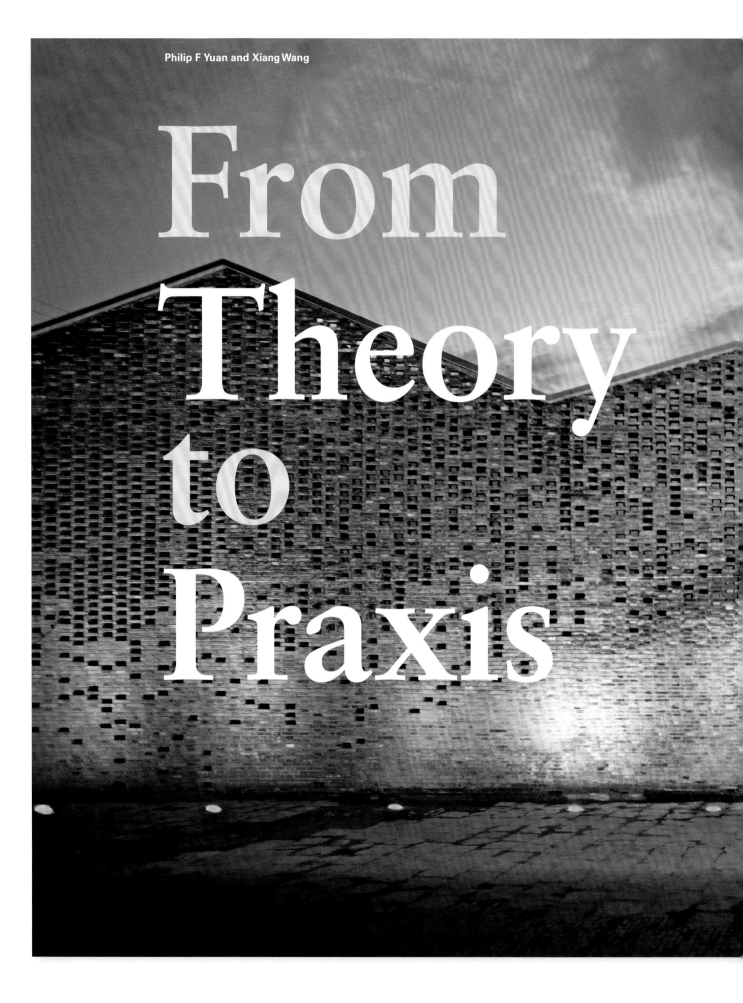

Philip F Yuan and Xiang Wang

From Theory to Praxis

Archi-Union Architects,
Pond Society (Chi She) exhibition
space renovation,
Shanghai,
2016

Recycled grey-green bricks salvaged from the old
building were chosen for the curved surface.

Digital Tools and the New Architectural Authorship

Archi-Union Architects, based in Shanghai, is an experimental practice that is closely linked to the Digital Design Research Center (DDRC) at Tongji University. The firm's founder **Philip F Yuan**, a professor at the university, together with his colleague and DDRC leader **Xiang Wang**, describe how their method of working as a design laboratory is enabling them to explore a new 'parametric regionalism' that marries digital techniques with traditional local materials and craftsmanship.

As Mario Carpo has argued, a relationship between architecture and its authorship that held sway from Alberti through to the rise of Modernism has been subverted in the digital era.[1] The variability inherent in digital design undermines an authorship that rests on conceptions of identity – of an architect's design and its built realisation, for example. This same variability, however, invites new perspectives on hand-crafted and culture-specific building traditions that have long been associated with the premodern. Many recent experimental parametric construction projects, especially in the Eastern world, demonstrate how culturally specific approaches to tectonics, materiality and the built environment can continue to play a critical role in architectural expression.

Current conditions inevitably lead to a reconsideration of authorship in architecture and to questions regarding the role of architects in the digital process. In the last 10 years, Archi-Union Architects has been employing advanced digital tools, such as algorithmic libraries and robotics-aided fabrication, in a practice that combines prototype research with comprehensive project execution. The result is a new authorship of tectonics, with a local adaptability made possible by digital technology.

Archi-Union Architects,
Exhibition of experimental
practice of the past 10 years,
Shanghai,
2017

The application of digital tools and the critical rethinking of the local context and craft traditions offer a path towards a new Chinese vernacular.

Experimental Integrated Prototypes

In the digital era, architectural design has experienced a great paradigm shift, away from traditional drafting techniques and towards systems of parametric components linked by tectonic logic.[2] These developments have been furthered by interdisciplinary initiatives that redefine the conception and execution of complexity in architectural design.

One result has been the rapid popularisation of experimental prototypes at full scale. Another has been a design method based on performance, as measured by the application of innovative analytic and algorithmic tools. The wealth of such digital tools has led to an architectural design process that approaches integrated scientific research. As Patrik Schumacher argues, now 'every design process includes a design research program'.[3] Archi-Union's practice has benefited greatly from these developments, especially insofar as they offer possibilities for a new understanding of traditional materials and structures, while the nonstandard serialisation of form makes complex geometry adaptable to traditional, low-tech materials and methods.

Another aspect, reflected particularly in Archi-Union's practice, is the use of advanced manufacturing techniques and digital fabrication in the design process. Robotics together with its associated information-technology networks provides an unprecedented interface between virtual spaces and real-world building processes. New physical capabilities can be explored using basic material parameters and digitally driven manufacturing and articulation techniques. New morphologies of the structure system can then be tested at full scale. In this way, design and construction are no longer separate, as they have been fused in a very early stage of the process.

The Digital in Chinese Culture

Although the globalisation of technology has made logic, algorithm and variation the common concern of contemporary architects everywhere, it is inevitable that the adaptability inherent to digital systems comes to play a role in their use in the local built environment. As architecture always exists in a physical and social context, regional resources, such as local customs and cultural heritage, have lately come to broaden the boundaries of parametricism and inform the digital design system. The resultant 'parametric regionalism', as it has been dubbed,[4] is a new departure in the era of digital design and manufacturing, one which finds a place for traditional materials, local craftsmanship and the architect's natural inheritance.

How digital tools and the new formalism they bring are employed reveals something of architects' attitudes towards the built environment. Since their advent in Archi-Union's design process, it has been the firm's fundamental belief that parametricism will be misconceived and misused if the design process is entirely tech-dominated.[5] The rapid digitalisation that has accompanied China's breakneck economic and industrial development has changed living habits and urban environments, with profound effects on the everyday life and physical and mental health of citizens. This has led to a great demand for renovated building traditions and structures and rejuvenating spaces.

A dialogue has arisen between developing technologies and Chinese architectural history, bringing new perspectives on traditional materials in the context of contemporary practice. Advanced manufacturing techniques also go hand in hand with the need to replace human labour as Chinese architecture and construction become more industrialised. Prefabricated building components, for example, can be not only mass-produced but also mass-customised. Over the past 10 years, Archi-Union has been devoted to pursuing the integration of digital manufacturing with local craftsmanship and materials, in this way bringing a strong regional character to very contemporary architectural design.[6]

DigitalFUTURES: the Catalyst for a New Architectural Authorship

Working as a design laboratory is the preferred mode for Archi-Union, and the studio has benefited from its experimental method. Theory and praxis, a combination of university-based architectural research and professional construction projects, find their natural connection through the application of digital tools. Archi-Union has a close association with the Digital Design Research Center (DDRC) at Tongji University, where construction problems are explored through the exploitation of digital tools and construction of full-scale prototypes. DDRC sponsors an annual workshop on digital design and manufacturing, named 'DigitalFUTURES', which typically culminates in a number of full-scale experimental pavilions built to test the architectural potential of digital tools. Through the professional projects implemented by Archi-Union, the established and tested workflow and algorithms that come of DDRC's research are applied to design with a concern for local materials, craftsmanship, context and climate.

Digital Design Research Center (DDRC),
Application of robotics
in experimental research,
Tongji University,
Shanghai,
2016

Experimentation with robotic fabrication has become an important tool in assessing new possibilities for traditional materials and craftsmanship in the digital era. Robotics is here being tested in large-scale fabrication of curved beam structures.

Brick Morphology

The Silk Wall project of 2009 (the facade design for Archi-Union's own studio) initiated a series of morphological designs in brick that explore digital design and fabrication as extensions of traditional, low-tech craftsmanship. Due to a lack of available tools for digital manufacture of brick, only a restricted repertoire of angles that would facilitate the rotation of the brick can be achieved, through a maximum of 21 distinct wood moulds. To bridge the gap between digital design and manufacture, experiments were conducted with the aim of exploiting the on-site robotic bricklaying technique. The geometric modelling and the control of the six-axis robot arm and mobile platform were established through research using full-scale prototypes. The fruits of these techniques can be seen in the renovation of the Pond Society (Chi She) exhibition space in Shanghai (2016), and it is the maturity of such digital tools that has inspired the architects to find new approaches to, and redefine the beauty of, traditional materials.

Archi-Union Architects,
Pond Society (Chi She) exhibition space renovation,
Shanghai,
2016

The complex facade form was fabricated with the robotic technique.

Digital Design
Research Center (DDRC),
Robotic Wall,
DigitalFUTURES workshop,
Tongji University,
Shanghai,
2014

Based on the Silk Wall experiments, a robotics-aided on-site fabrication technique was developed.

Robotic band-saw techniques are here being tested for large-scale prefabrication.

An efficient ribbed-shell structure was built with the digital manufacturing techniques developed for large-scale curved beams.

Performative Tectonics in Timber

In addition to its innovative revisiting of traditional materials and craftsmanship, Archi-Union's prototype-based design research has brought fresh thinking to structural design, with a combination of traditional structural morphology and robotic manufacturing that the firm has dubbed 'Structural Performative Tectonics'.[7]

For the timber tectonics shell design project for DigitalFUTURES 2016, a performance-oriented design was researched and tested. Exploration of form, structural optimisation and connection systems, as well as manufacturing techniques were combined in a digital design based on plug-ins such as RhinoVAULT and Millepede. Meanwhile, a robotic band-saw cutting technique was tested on full-scale prefabricated components. The conception was realised in the Timber Structure Theme Pavilion at the 2016 Jiangsu Horticultural Expo in Suzhou (the largest gridshell pavilion at the expo), which demonstrated the feasibility and efficiency of the design to the prefabricated architecture industry.

The advantages of digital tools for nonstandard prefabrication are also seen in the recent project In-Bamboo (2017), a community centre for a village in Chongzhou. Totally prefabricated, the whole building took only 65 days to construct. The curved and interlocking form conceptualises 'infinity', and its form, also alluding to local weaving crafts, again demonstrates the warp and woof of the digital and the traditional in the architects' understanding of form, material and structure. As one writer has said, In-Bamboo 'elegantly makes the case for a symbiotic relationship among rural, industrial, and digital'.[8]

Archi-Union's prototype-based design research has brought fresh thinking to structural design

Archi-Union Architects,
Timber Structure
Theme Pavilion,
Jiangsu Horticultural Expo,
Suzhou,
Jiangsu province,
2016

The first large-scale non-uniform timber shell structure in China, developed through the combination of performance-based design and robotic fabrication.

Authorship is increasingly expressed through the attitudes architects adopt towards the possibilities of melding technology and tradition.

Archi-Union Architects,
In-Bamboo community cultural centre,
Chongzhou,
Chengdu,
Sichuan province,
2017

above: The application of digital tools to the local context and craftsmanship enabled the fast construction of the floating roof.

The interlocked curved roof forms the symbol for infinity and creates a continuous space for the public interactions.

An Emerging Digital Vernacular

These working methods and projects illustrate Archi-Union's attempts to integrate digital design with the Chinese vernacular. Digital tools rooted in an understanding of materials are freeing architects from the technological limitations of the past and leading to new design methodologies capable of incorporating traditional craftsmanship and adapting to the local culture. Authorship is increasingly expressed through the attitudes architects adopt towards the possibilities of melding technology and tradition. Material-based performative tectonics is in this regard powerfully expressive, and points the way towards a new regionalism.[9] ⌀

Notes
1. Mario Carpo, *The Alphabet and the Algorithm*, MIT Press (Cambridge, MA), 2011.
2. Philip F Yuan, 'Digital Fabrication Paradigm Shifting Under the New Methodology', *Time Architecture*, 111 (3), 2012, pp 288–94.
3. Patrik Schumacher, *The Autopoiesis of Architecture, Volume I: A New Framework for Architecture*, John Wiley & Sons (Chichester), 2011.
4. Philip F Yuan, 'Parametric Regionalism', in Patrik Schumacher (ed), ⌀ *Parametricism 2.0: Rethinking Architecture's Agenda for the 21st Century*, no 2 (March/April), 2016. pp 92–9.
5. Philip F Yuan and Lingfei Pan, 'Silk Wall: Thinking and Practice on Parametric Tectonic Design', *Urbanism & Architecture*, 6, 2010.
6. Antoine Picon, *Digital Culture in Architecture: An Introduction for the Design Professions*, Birkhäuser (Basel), 2011.
7. Philip F Yuan, Hao Meng and Pradeep Devadass, 'Performative Tectonics', in Wes McGee and Monica Ponce de Leon (eds), *Robotic Fabrication in Architecture, Art and Design 2014*, Springer (New York), 2014, pp 181–95.
8. Aric Chen, 'A Twist on Tradition: A Community Center in a Rural Village Brings Dynamism to the Vernacular', *Architectural Record*, February 2018.
9. This article is funded by the National Natural Science Foundation of China (Grant No 51578378), the Special Funds for State Key R&D Program during the 13th Five-Year Plan Period of China (Grant No 2016YFC0702104) and the Sino-German Center Research Program (Grant No GZ1162).

In-Bamboo provides a new paradigm for traditional construction and illustrates a rethinking of the task of rural revitalisation in China.

Lighting Architec
A Collaborative

Tiantian Xu / DnA Design and Architecture (architecture),
Xin Zhang / X Studio,
School of Architecture,
Tsinghua University (lighting strategy),
Brown Sugar Workshop,
Songyang,
Zhejiang province,
China,
2016

With the background of the dark ceiling and the steam rising up during the sugar-making process, the lighting concept is materialised in the form of 'light gates'.

Led ture

Approach

Xin Zhang

The common practice of leaving lighting design until last may be diminishing architectural potential. **Xin Zhang**, who teaches and leads a research team at Tsinghua University, has been exploring ways of using lighting concepts to inform the formulation of architectural ideas since 2009. His experience through his work with various architects shows how involving lighting engineers from the initial phases of design can greatly enhance the atmospheric qualities of built projects.

The practice of professional lighting design originates from stage lighting, dating back to the Renaissance.[1] The goal of stage lighting design is to present scenery and actors in a three-dimensional space in a way that induces the audience to think and to feel immersed in the scene. For designers, the priority is to carefully analyse the script but not participate in the writing process.

The field of architectural lighting design originated in the US in the 1950s and eventually became associated with the works of modernist masters. The most significant illustration is the collaboration between the pioneering American lighting designer Richard Kelly, known as 'the father of modern architectural lighting', and famous modernist architects, such as Mies van der Rohe for the Seagram Building in New York City (1958) or Louis Kahn for the Kimbell Art Museum in Fort Worth, Texas (1972). Architectural lighting gradually formed a design methodology different from stage lighting. For example, Kelly carefully avoided the use of coloured light or strong contrasts between light and shadow, and emphasised that visual emotion should be planned on the basis of the function of the space. His lasting contribution to modern architecture includes successfully hiding lighting fixtures and carefully planning the luminance relationship of every reflective surface.[2]

Despite almost 70 years of cooperation between architects and lighting designers, an issue that still affects architects is daylight, which has been incorporated into the formal consideration of architectural typology. The contribution of artificial light is now regarded as a slightly tiresome necessity.[3] In the process of working with architects, lighting designers have been in a subordinate position. Even the greatest ones emphasise the importance of advice from architects, such as Mies van der Rohe's, Louis Kahn's and Philip Johnson's to Richard Kelly, or Arata Isozaki's and Toyo Ito's to Kaoru Mende. The influence of lighting designers on architects is seldom documented.

Architectural lighting research has focused on the relationship between lighting and visual tasks, while there has been less research linking light with space and behaviour. The latter, such as lighting designer, educator and author Christopher Cuttle's proposal of using space as a secondary light source, quantifies how primary light sources, such as windows and lamps, ultimately lead light directly into human eyes in the space.[4] The long-standing gap between research objectives and design goals has hindered the impact of lighting on architectural practice.

Design and consultancy work are not only about how architecture is presented but also the original architectural conception, including visual images, spatial organisation and construction logic. The architectural design process needs to be improved, to apply the concept of lighting to all of its stages. In cooperation with several top-tier architects in China, my team has integrated lighting into design practice. Through a series of research-based designs – six of which are described and illustrated here – various ways have been found to promote the architectural value of light.

The team's working method embraces five key aspects. The first of these is incorporating light intent into an architectural design concept that uses the visual image as the origin. Second is achieving a synergy of light and spatial composition, as well as functional organisation, for the visual logic of the building. Third is placing basic visual tasks in the context of architecture to re-examine and create grand narratives in everyday life. Fourth is incorporating light sources into the construction logic to achieve a fusion – giving light to shape, and giving shape to light. The last aspect is quantitatively interpreting architects' philosophy of daylight design to achieve architect-specific daylight goals.

The Golden Haystack

The Vanke Pavilion for Expo 2010 in Shanghai was designed by Duo Xiang Studio. The structure consisted of three upright cones and four inverted cones with a skin of straw boards. Transparent ETFE sheeting forms a connecting roof. The interiors of the cones feature independent exhibition halls and logistics offices, and the exterior is surrounded by a landscaped pool.

The core idea of daylight design was identified at the outset – namely, daylight autonomy, shadow performance, and seeing blue sky. My team here visualised and provided the quantitative design criteria using research methods to create a mock-up and analysis for the daylight system, thus helping the architects to complete the design.

Anticipating an excessive quantity of LEDs at Expo 2010, a low-key design strategy was chosen: the functional lighting in the atrium space was provided by the reflected light from the cylindrical surface. In the outer space, light overflowed between the cylinders, leaving the cylinder facades in silhouette. It offered a welcome 'reef' in the 'LED ocean' featured at the Shanghai Expo.

Xiang Lu / Duo Xiang Studio (architecture),
Xin Zhang / X Studio,
School of Architecture,
Tsinghua University (lighting strategy),
Vanke Pavilion,
Expo 2010,
Shanghai,
2010

A low-key lighting design strategy was chosen. The functional lighting in the atrium space was given by the reflection of light from the cylindrical surfaces, which were illuminated by lighting fixtures hidden in the coving above the doors of other cylinders.

Tiantian Xu / DnA Design and Architecture (architecture),
Xin Zhang / X Studio, School of Architecture,
Tsinghua University (lighting strategy),
Brown Sugar Factory,
Songyang,
Zhejiang province,
China,
2016

The Light Gate

Completed in 2016 by architect Tiantian Xu of DnA Design and Architecture, the Brown Sugar Factory is situated between farmland and a tea plantation in Songyang, Zhejiang province. For villagers, it is a processing workshop; for tourists, it is a museum that showcases traditional sugar-making techniques. As a performance and exhibition venue, the workshop highlights the cultural tradition of the village.

The lighting concept plays an important role in strengthening the dramatic and experimental characteristics of this space. It creates an experiential relationship between the sugar makers, the visitors and the rural landscape.

With the background of a dark ceiling and steam rising up during the sugar-making process, the lighting is materialised into a series of 'light gates'. By increasing the contrast between light and dark, sugar-making scenes are presented as a theatrical performance. Visitors walk in the dark, but as they approach the sugar-processing area, they are lit up and become participants in the live show.

left: Peripheral circulation space is divided by double-glazed curtain walls. Light plays a role in strengthening the dramatic and experimental characteristics of the space, creating an experience of openness between sugar makers, visitors and the rural landscape.

below: By increasing the contrast between light and dark, the lighting strategy presents sugar-making scenes as if they were in a theatre or museum. Visitors walk in darkness, but once they are close to the sugar-processing area, they are lit up and become participants and performers in the live show.

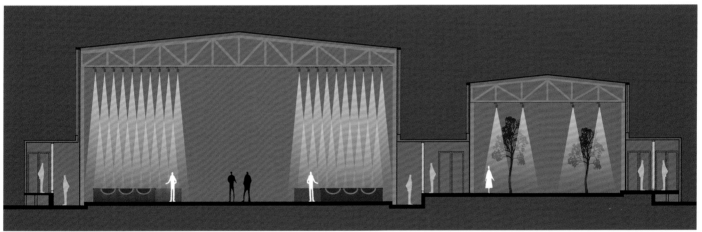

Visitors walk in the dark, but as they approach the sugar-processing area, they are lit up and become participants in the live show.

Giving Light to Shape

For the 2014 Venice Architecture Biennale, the exhibition in the Chinese Pavilion was called 'Mountains Beyond Mountains', which describes a relationship between modernity and traditional Chinese philosophy.

The three main materials used corresponded to three prefabricated and assembled systems: a light steel supporting system as the spatial truss structure; waste wrapping plates for pedestals, furniture and rockeries; and bandages as coverings for the walls and roofs. Light was the fourth material, and although it was less obvious, it had an effect on the selection of structural design and covering materials.

Through close cooperation with Duo Xiang Studio, light was integrated seamlessly within the architectural framework and furniture, and also converted the structures into lamps. Walls displaying paintings were backlit; screen lamps separated spaces on the tables; stool lamps were used as steps or furniture; and construction materials and approaches, such as light steel systems and elastic bandages, were made into screen lamps, in keeping with the traditional Chinese wooden structures of architecture and furniture.

Xiang Lu / Duo Xiang Studio (architecture),
Xin Zhang / X Studio, School of Architecture,
Tsinghua University (lighting strategy),
Chinese Pavilion,
14th Venice Architecture Biennale,
Venice,
Italy,
2014

right: Linear diffused light comes down from the roof to punctuate the space. It highlights some focal points, indicates direction, separates areas of the space and creates depth and atmosphere.

below: Light integrates with architectural frameworks and furniture, converting them into lamps and then adding functions beyond lighting: walls bearing paintings are backlit; screen lamps separate spaces on tables.

He Wei / 3andwich Design / He Wei Studio (architecture),
Xin Zhang / X Studio, School of Architecture,
Tsinghua University (lighting strategy),
Papa's Hostel,
Songyang,
Zhejiang province,
China,
2015

Soft Shining Boxes

The origins of Papa's Hostel lie in an ordinary two-storey rammed-earth dwelling in Songyang, Zhejiang province. The architects He Wei Studio transformed the building into a youth hostel in 2015, renovating the space and offering it a new function and youth appeal.

Several spatial elements were introduced into the house, creating 'rooms within rooms'. The spaces are made from lightweight materials, which are dismountable, portable and translucent. The design for the lighting strengthens the characteristics of the interior space. By placing the linear LED fixtures in a wooden framework, they are transformed into soft shining boxes of light. When warm white light is switched on, it is sweet and dreamy; on the contrary, when coloured light is switched on, it creates a feeling of excitement.

The relationship between the light and hollow sheets is based on a full-scale model experiment, in which the direction of the light was perpendicular to the hollow sheet cavity. The lighting composition is full of artistic expression, and the light sources can be looked at directly, which is apt for the youthful characteristics of a hostel.

Soft linear LEDs (both warm white and coloured) are placed in the wooden framework of the 'rooms within rooms'. The light composition is artistic and expressive, and the light sources can be looked at directly – fitting the 'young' profile of the youth hostel.

Linear LED fixtures are placed in the wooden framework of the 'rooms within rooms', making them into soft shining boxes of light. The electricity for each room box comes from the floor plug under it, the wire being left long enough to guarantee an electrical supply when the room box is moved.

The lighting composition is full of artistic expression, and the light sources can be looked at directly, which is apt for the youthful characteristics of a hostel.

The Torch

Also in Songyang is the Hakka Indenture Museum, completed in 2017 and built with local natural stones, which have been integrated into the mountain terrain. The design, by Tiantian Xu, symbolises the honest and trustworthy 'spirit of indenture' which is firmly rooted in the area. The aim in collaborating with the architect was to transform the museum into a local landmark and to attract tourists to explore the vanishing traditional local culture. At the same time, the design guides the concept of rural lighting and how it can be improved gradually while also protecting the 'dark' experience.

Inspired by local residents' use of fire torches in traditional celebrations, the designers came up with the concept of a 'torch'. Sunken low-energy LED uplights are placed along the narrow side of the stone walls, appearing like rows of torches. This aesthetic sense of order is integrated with local characteristics. Surface-mounted downlights outline the doorways and guide people to visit and walk through the space.

Tiantian Xu / DnA Design and Architecture (architecture),
Xin Zhang / X Studio,
School of Architecture,
Tsinghua University (lighting strategy),
Hakka Indenture Museum,
Songyang,
Zhejiang province,
2017

The 'torch' lighting concept was inspired by the traditional celebratory use of fire torches by local residents. The sunken low-energy LED uplights light the narrow sides of the stone walls, symbolising series of 'torches'.

Inspired by local residents' use of fire torches in traditional celebrations, the designers came up with the concept of a 'torch'.

Surface-mounted downlights outline the shapes of doors and guide people to visit and walk through. Layers of doors make the architectural space much deeper.

The Colourful Tyndall Effect

The Tobacco-Curing House is an ancient village renovation project in Shangping village, Fujian province, completed in 2017. The architects He Wei Studio selected a number of abandoned agricultural facilities and pieces of infrastructure in the village for renovation. The lighting design is in keeping with the location of the building, which protects the natural and dark environment of the village, but creates well-timed surprises by adding interesting and artistic modern design to this traditional atmosphere.

An innovative skylight features coloured acrylic plates that appear to be placed at random, but are in fact carefully arranged. Sunlight is intensified by the coloured light from this skylight, creating a Tyndall effect (whereby light is scattered as it passes through a colloid). In order to form a perfect natural rainbow effect, the order and the widths of the light colours were determined through numerous field experiments.

Mirrors are placed carefully on the interior beams to reflect the coloured shadows throughout all parts of the house. The lighting design helped the architects achieve the concept of what they describe as 'a ritual place for people to reconsider the relationship between man and nature'.

He Wei,
3andwich Design / He Wei Studio (architecture),
Xin Zhang / X Studio,
School of Architecture,
Tsinghua University (lighting strategy),
Tobacco-Curing House in Shangping Village Regeneration,
Jianning county,
Fujian province,
China,
2017

In the tobacco-curing house, the lighting design features an innovative skylight device. The sunlight is refracted by coloured acrylic, giving a 'Tyndall effect'.

The Lighting Designer's Role

What is unique about my team's work is how it enhances the involvement of lighting designers in architectural design decisions and helps their voices to be heard.

Through long-term collaboration, evaluation criteria were established with the different architects to align with each firm's qualities. In addition to the process of participation, the lighting designers summarised the pros and cons of each project, including articles, awards, and patents for fixtures. The contributions of the lighting designers helped the architectural firms make lighting an important aspect of the architectural concept and enabled them to innovate continuously, while gradually developing different lighting styles.

Because of the particularity of light, and especially the dynamic and regional nature of daylight, current design and communication tools – including renderings, calculation software, mock-ups and virtual reality – have some drawbacks when making auxiliary lighting decisions. Therefore, a summary of these experiences remains crucial. With improved tools, and by narrowing the gap between research and practice in lighting, there are ever-greater prospects for lighting-led architecture. ⌀

Notes
1. Linda Essig, *Lighting and the Design Idea*, Thomson Wadsworth (Belmont), second edition, 2005, p 1.
2. Dietrich Neumann, *The Structure of Light*, Yale University Press (New Haven, CT and London), 2010, p 3.
3. Kevin Mansfield, 'Architectural Lighting Design Review: The Past 50 Years', *Lighting Research and Technology* 50, 2018, pp 80–97.
4. Christopher Cuttle, 'Towards the Third Stage of the Lighting Profession', *Lighting Research and Technology* 42, 2010, pp 73–90.

Architecture as Synthetic Agency

Andong Lu

LanD Studio,
'Instant Garden'
exhibition,
Nanjing Folk Museum,
Nanjing,
2017

Architectural elements, doors, windows, passages, caves etc divided and reunited this ephemeral garden space. This installation used a video camera and a wireless projector to mirror the image of the female dancer's performance (within the moon-gate) onto the wall at the opposite side of the courtyard, where a male dancer performed against simulacrum.

Narrative-Augmented Design in Practice

LanD Studio is a Nanjing-based think-tank for place-making that carries out design research in real conditions. Guest-Editor **Andong Lu**, who co-founded the studio with fellow former Cambridge University researcher and Guest-Editor Pingping Dou, introduces its form of working through recent installations and interventions that embrace architectural renovation, exhibitions, participatory performance and mass-media activities. Architecture here becomes a meaningful experience that connects people to each other and to their environment.

The literati gardens of China epitomise an age-old notion of place that is different from the European notion of the genius loci. It is not bound to a fixed location (therefore protecting and representing that location), but rather in the manner of what might be called augmented reality. In a Chinese garden, the experience of being *in situ* becomes the evidence of narrative images (often with visual-textual clues), and – through a process not unlike a game of make-believe – people transcend the here-and-now to achieve a cultural empathy via ideals which they share with their ancestors. Experiencing is therefore both imagining and participating, and the situation becomes the agency for the dual experience of culture and embodiment. This kind of narrative-augmented place is generally considered as superior to merely natural places. Through cultural transcription of the physical world, it leaves sufficient space for the engagement of the human mind.

Secluded Pavilion of Parasol Tree and Bamboo,
Humble Administrator's Garden,
Suzhou,
1870s

Located near the literati garden's central pond, this pavilion is encircled by four moon-gates, which create an illusionary effect. Sitting among these, the visitor is secluded from the external world which is reflected in four 'mirrors', and his/her solitude is consoled by the natural friends of parasol tree and bamboo, planted to the north.

This notion of place obviously challenges the established understanding of architecture as a replete object of design. Here what is to be built is part of a more inclusive scheme of design that integrates built form with other non-visual forms, such as sound, scent or textual clues. It delivers through the synthesis of mediums, rather like a video with a voiceover, a more explicitly articulated immersive experience. Not only is built form an inseparable part of a larger design scheme, but synthesised form performs as an agency rather than a monument. This is a different kind of architecture, and it requires a different understanding of design.

LanD Studio regards 'narrative-augmented place' and 'synthetic agency' as key issues of investigation in contemporary architecture. These issues underpin a humanistic approach to integrating digitality within a built environment that puts poetics, meaning and social interaction at the core of design. Since its foundation in 2012, LanD Studio has conducted government consultation projects, studio teaching, exhibitions and public participation projects to redefine the role of architecture in the meaningful production of space.

It delivers through the synthesis of mediums, rather like a video with a voiceover, a more explicitly articulated immersive experience.

LanD Studio,
Renovation proposal
for the Contemplative Hall,
Memorial Hall of the
Victims in Nanjing Massacre
by Japanese Invaders,
Nanjing,
2018

This proposal involves renovating the existing Contemplative Hall by applying a new inner skin incorporating a matrix of sensors that respond to the visitor's act of contemplation (standing still for 30 seconds) by brightening up the space accordingly. As more visitors engage in contemplation, the hall will turn from a cold and gloomy space into a light and consoling atmosphere.

Moving images of courtyards were projected onto the original courtyards, to create a hybrid space. The original residential complex was built in the early 19th century.

Reconfiguring Reality

'Instant Garden' is an exhibition of spatial installations that explores the reconfiguration of reality in the Chinese garden. Undertaken in the historical courtyards of Xi Gan's Residence (now Nanjing Folk Museum) in April 2017, this project experimented with filmic projections to transform the classical courtyards into narrative-augmented reality, in an approach similar to traditional garden-making. The moving images overlapped a possible space onto real space and created juxtapositions of the present and the imagined, of concealing and revealing. Dancers were invited to make use of the architectural elements, doors, windows, passages and caves, in both real and projected spaces and establish inventive relationships between those elements. The dancers' physically present bodies and their images in the projected space interacted with each other, which on one hand created narrative relationships such as a stroll from the present into the illusion, and on the other hand served as props that drew visitors into the augmented reality. For the visitor, the built form (here the existing courtyards) framed the body, while the moving image performed a role similar to textual clues in a garden – that is, to focus attention onto certain selected dimensions and relationships within the setting, and therefore better articulate and elaborate them.

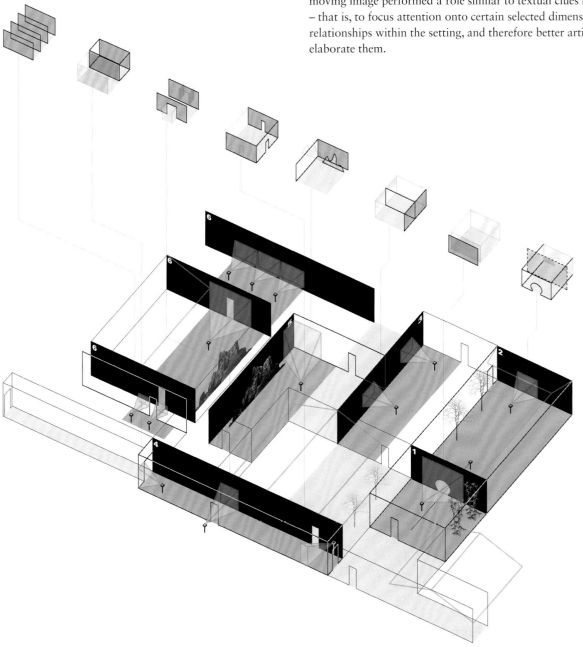

Transcriptive Design

Instead of the immersive experience of 'narrative-augmented place' in the 'Instant Garden' project, the Ephemera project explored another prototype: networked places. Ephemera was a proposal for a model renovation scheme for Tangshu village, Rulin town, commissioned in 2013 by the Jiangsu Provincial Department of Housing and Urban-Rural Development. In this project, LanD Studio addressed the worsening issue of the loss of identity in rural areas during mass urbanisation. Instead of transplanting a presumed vernacular style onto the village, the project centred on a series of 'transcriptions' to create a narrative-augmented agency, which formulated a new kind of spatial relationship between a communal centre and a village.

Firstly, Ephemera conducted micro-interventions into the staging of everyday objects in place. Each object was given a matrix barcode that allowed it to 'narrate' the everyday memories it afforded. As such, the everyday object was transcribed into an ephemera with a life story, a performer and a narrator of a specific place. The matrix barcode also enabled the second tier of transcription – through archiving, networking and mapping – to build up narrative links between the ephemeras. Now the place network of the village was indexed by a landscape of things. When an ephemera 'died', or ceased functioning, it was transferred to the community centre located at the entrance of the village. This architecture displayed the everyday artefacts underpinning local history, which invited visitors to retrace their original places scattered in the village for exploration. Embedded in domesticity and everydayness, the ephemeras were exceptional catalysts of engagement that invited people to play and read. The stratum of ephemeras connected architecture to places and turned the village into a multi-fold indexed site of memory. In this project, digitality enabled the 'transcriptive' design.

The community centre proposal is simultaneously a 'cabinet of curiosities', an index to places of interest in the village, and a natural starting point of exploration. The architecture symbolises the community in a new way.

LanD Studio,
Ephemera,
Tangshu village,
Jiangsu province,
2013

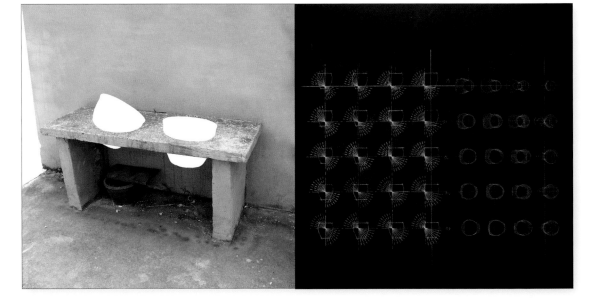

The micro-intervention involves the design of the staging of everyday objects to make them both accessible to villagers and revealing to visitors. It needed to carefully reconcile the conflict between everyday use and meaningful presentation.

LanD Studio,
Memory Project of the Nanjing Yangtze River Bridge,
Nanjing,
2017

For the sub-project *Everyone Owns the Bridge for Three Minutes*,
LanD Studio collaborated with social media firm Tencent. Eighteen
groups from near and far were invited to be filmed performing creative
activities on top of the landmark and under a temporary pavilion
designed by LanD Studio. The event was broadcast online and watched
by 100,000 people simultaneously.

The sub-project *Wiki-memory* is a portable installation that can be
recomposed flexibly. The prefabricated units are sized according
to the final exhibition hall. The 320 cubes are allocated to four
rotatable clusters of shelves. When the clusters are put together,
they enclose a contemplative courtyard surrounded by polished
stainless-steel walls.

Narrative Architecture

The Nanjing Yangtze River Bridge was the most well-known
icon of the Cultural Revolution and a national symbol of
1960s–1970s China. Different from traditional monuments, it
was overwhelmingly disseminated in mass media and had an
extensive presence in people's everyday lives nationwide. In 2014,
LanD Studio initiated the Memory Project of the Nanjing Yangtze
Bridge, together with a group of humanities scholars and local
artists, to use this exceptional source of collective memory as a
catalyst to reclaim this ideological monument as contemporary
public space. In the past four years, the Memory Project firstly
collected and archived the abundant memories around this
historical landmark and then, by collaborating with mass media
and social media (China Central Television, Tencent etc) and
conducting public talks, exhibitions and participatory activities,
gradually redefined the icon. As the project's influence grew, LanD
Studio received the commission to renovate the bridge tower into
a museum of memory, to be completed in late 2018.

The project's design strategy focused on the agency role of
artefacts and images in creating a narrative architecture that
brought forth the visitor's process of participation. Similar to
Ephemera, this project used 'objects of memory' as an index
between architecture and larger public space. On the other hand,
due to its once exceptional media coverage and the ritualised
ways of photographing it, images of the bridge, associated
with the point of view of an ideally placed observer, became an
extraordinary agency of spatio-visual memory.

As a sub-project of the Memory Project, *Wiki-memory* is a
crowd-funded 'portable' installation that was first exhibited at
the Shanghai Urban Space Art Season (Shanghai, October 2017
to January 2018), then at the Jiangsu Art Museum (Nanjing,
September to December 2018), before finally being assembled
into an exhibition hall inside the bridge museum. It comprises 320
cubes that connect the future museum (under construction) to the
digital database of memories. Each cube has a customised matrix
barcode allowing visitors to scan to explore the stories lying
behind. Five types of narrative threads – temporal, geographical,
thematic, biographical and interactive – were designed that
directed the visitor from one cube to another. Here the objects on
display are regarded as triggers of memory, through which visitors
can enter into and explore the digitised landscape of memories,
while the index system allows them to locate any material
'evidences' during the navigation. This design targets a new
prototype of narrative architecture, in which spatial experience
and online navigation are independent but mutually indexed.
The visitor is no longer a receiver of a singular narrative, but
an explorer who builds up a memory from her/his own trajectory
of engagement.

Architecture in the Age of Digital Humanism

How does the traditional notion of place as narrative-augmented
reality inform contemporary architecture and urbanism?
In an age of burgeoning digitality and humanism, the discipline
of architecture has to extend beyond its traditional tectonic scope
to better serve as an agency that connects people to nature,
meaning and others. This calls for a new understanding of
architecture, and digitality has a major role to play in design
towards synthetic agency. ⌂

Pingping Dou, Andong Lu and Lu Feng

Imagining the Immediate Present

Responsive Approaches to the Investigation of Things

Keyang Tang,
Objego,
Gewu Workshop,
Nanjing,
2015

The anonymous objects found through collective scavenging underpinned a revealing process in which multiple egos built up individual connections with the site. Here, a genuine understanding of the site only emerged out of the archipelago of meanings in an ocean of things.

Grand theories cannot always provide the answer to local problems. In line with a tenet of neo-Confucian philosophy, Guest-Editors **Pingping Dou and Andong Lu** and architect and researcher **Lu Feng** together co-convened the Gewu Workshop in Nanjing in summer 2015 to showcase different types of enquiry. The 10 invited participants, ranging from architects to historians and theorists, each offered their analysis of and vision for a disused area on the outskirts of historic Nanjing. Displayed in a subsequent exhibition, their proposals encourage an investigative and place-based mentality in dealing with such complex urban sites.

Conducted in the old town of Nanjing in the summer of 2015, the aim of the Gewu Workshop was to set the future agenda of responsive design research in China, focusing on alternative contexts in which methods, roles and definitions need to be re-examined. As part of a collective design experiment, 10 leading young practitioners from diverse professional backgrounds (architects, architectural historians, theorists, a curator and a journal editor) were invited to carry out research studies on a common site in the Hualugang district. The rationale for the selection was to include as many of the different types of enquiry employed in contemporary Chinese architecture as possible. Instead of proposals for future urban development, however, the workshop focused on a series of exercises to interrogate and imagine the present.

The complexity and contradictions in urbanising China raise questions as to the validity of grand theories and methodologies. Responsible practitioners need to undertake first-hand investigations to find solutions to local problems. In this context, traditional task-driven practice through the application of general design principles is increasingly being superseded by emerging forms of design practice characterised by more specific and systematic enquiries. Such investigations can only come from an understanding of the present. The workshop therefore adopted the neo-Confucian philosophy of the 'investigation of things' (*gewu*),[1] calling for attention to design as a discerning, appropriate response rather than self-expression.

A Specific Any-Place

The complex site in the peripheral area of the old town in Nanjing, at the inner edge of the city wall, had become a tabula rasa over the last decade, but once included an abundance of natural, historical and modern elements: a legendary tower on the site was portrayed in a famous poem of the 8th century; traces of ancient tombs and temples can still be found; and the remains of the 14th-century city wall protected 19th-century houses and gardens that were replaced piecemeal by modern factories in the mid-20th century. Today this collaged landscape is a void, an any-place of urban China, waiting for investigation. It represents the Chinese urban condition, but is simultaneously defamiliarised from the everyday. Is it really a tabula rasa? How can its immediate present be understood? Combined, the different perspectives of the workshop proposals constructed the answer to these questions: the site is both an uncertain testing ground to be discovered, and an invention of the individual investigations.

Investigation as Response

Prior to the workshop, and unaware of the investigation site, the invited 'investigators' were asked to propose a distinctive modus operandi, a summary of their previous studies or practice and hence reflecting a long-term standpoint. Each then led a team of assistants in applying their proposed approach to a study of the common site. Seminars were held at the beginning, middle and end of the workshop during which the investigators were asked to present how their design proposals had been developed through the ongoing investigation to an audience of invited scholars and editors – a stimulating intellectual context that encouraged them to conduct both research and reflection at the same time. Here the focus was not the tools or methods used in the investigation, but ways of responding to frame, define and integrate the various design issues. In requiring the investigators to respond to a common context and to meet common challenges, the workshop became a meta-project, a platform for testing and sharing 10 parallel working methods.

The Investigation of Things

Investigators were encouraged to develop theoretical hypotheses and elaborate on these through argumentative design. They faced both external challenges and internal quests. Some paid more attention to ways of seeing, while others focused more on ways of working.

Xinggang Li (pp 16–23), chief architect of the China Architecture Design & Research Group, tested his long-term research agenda on 'scenery and geometry' on the Nanjing site. Based on the capacity of scaffolding to be rapidly erected or removed, his *Instant Arcadia* installation demonstrated multiple ways to install it to re-create the form and structure of traditional architectural typologies and reclaim the site as a temporary poetic space.

In *Archaeology of Space*, Yao Ding, an architectural historian from Tianjin University, criticised the dichotomous ways of thinking (for example, historical versus the present) that undermine the wholeness of a site, and proposed an alternative interpretation that, through the reiterative investigation of things, gradually exposed existing connections and revealed the site as a unified reality.

Xinggang Li,
Instant Arcadia,
Gewu Workshop,
Nanjing,
2015

above and top: Li used standard scaffolding and shade cloth to fabricate four temporary structures – a hall on a terrace, a tree pavilion, a corridor along the city wall and a tower by an artificial mountain – to redefine existing elements and reclaim the site as an imagined garden.

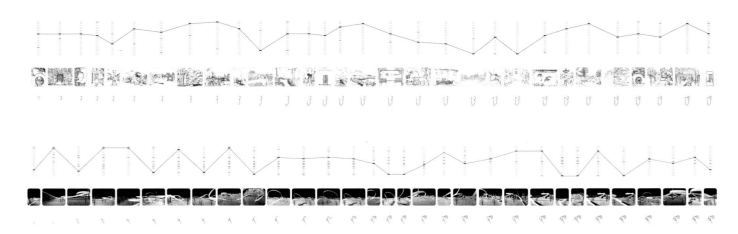

Li Zhang,
Playfulness,
Gewu Workshop,
Nanjing,
2015

The two diagrams chart the undulating experience of movement within the historical Yu Garden (above) and during the proposed remapping of the site (below).

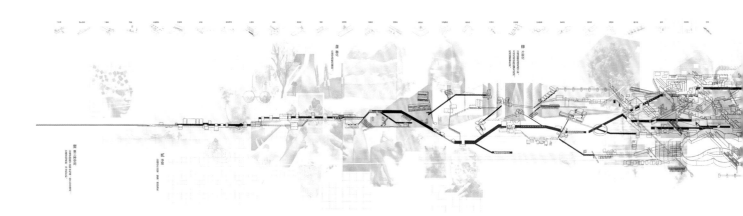

Andong Lu,
Cloud Wall,
Gewu Workshop,
Nanjing,
2015

Visualisation of the evolution (from left to right) of the wall as architecture (thick wall), garden (forked wall), urbanism (folded wall) and finally a strategic proposal for the regeneration of the site. The *Cloud Wall* can be envisioned by juxtaposing diagrams with interpretative resources.

Yao Ding, *Archaeology of Space*,
'Investigate It' exhibition,
OCT Contemporary Art Terminal – OCAT Shanghai,
2016

For the special exhibition on the Gewu Workshop investigations, Yao Ding reinterpreted the reality of the site in an installation consisting of present and absent images to be deciphered and unified through the 'archaeology of space'.

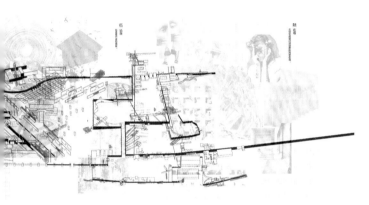

Keyang Tang, a renowned curator and writer, devised the concept of *Objego* (an abbreviation of object-ego) to epitomise an exercise in which a group of students undertook a massive scavenger hunt of the site for human leftovers – plural 'objects' – which resulted in an ocean of individual speculations generated by their collective 'egos'. Without conditions or premises, the project did not conform to any obvious structure, but revealed the open nature of the site, like an archipelago gradually emerging in unknown waters.

Architectural theorist Andong Lu reflected on modern conceptions of object-based and locus-based space. A Chinese spatial prototype of dichromatic participation, his *Cloud Wall* was characterised by assimilation and syllepsis, inhabiting a place through referencing and borrowing manifested as a series of narratives. A manifesto was then produced and tested to devise an urban design for the Nanjing site.

In *Boundary Mapping*, Ling Zhou, a university-based architect, used textual criticism to identify the boundaries of disappeared buildings and gardens on the site from historical documents. The final product was a set of boundary maps, a quasi-proposal for future urban design and preservation. The regulated format of traditional Chinese architecture, with its unidentical orthogonal columnar grid, also enabled an exemplary design proposal for the restoration of the site.

In *Playfulness*, Li Zhang, an architect and editor (and author of the 'Counterpoint' article in this issue – see pp 134–41), teased the lack of human feeling in architectural practice, arguing that pleasure needs to be realised and obtained through bodily practice. The project first mapped the abundant experience of playfulness in the case of the site's 19th-century Yu Garden, in terms of movement, visibility, bodily relations and the interstitial. It then proposed a method of remapping playfulness in which the site was designed according to bodily practice.

Architect Bin Zhang defined architectural practice as an expression of existence and as an intervention in social production. His *Urban Farm Reclusion* envisioned the potential of piecemeal redevelopment of leftover or deserted urban land and the temporary occupancy of urban public space as a low-cost development model, a cultural settlement of hybrid self-constructed functional units of various scales in the form of an urban village.

Jiang Feng, an architectural historian, used a ladder as a metaphor to connect things with what lies beyond them, arguing that there are profound hidden gaps in the understanding of a site, and it is only human imagination that can eventually bridge those gaps. His *Ladder* project thus informs, instructs and extends our imagination to the past and afar.

Ling Zhou,
Boundary Mapping,
Gewu Workshop,
Nanjing,
2015

Using layered mapping of the boundaries of historical places (present or demolished) on the site, the architect created a collaged landscape of imagined restoration.

For *Translucency*, his team investigated four
notable elements of the site – the city wall, Yu
Garden, industrial buildings and residential blocks
– and analysed how these urban elements became
translucent through certain spatial strategies.

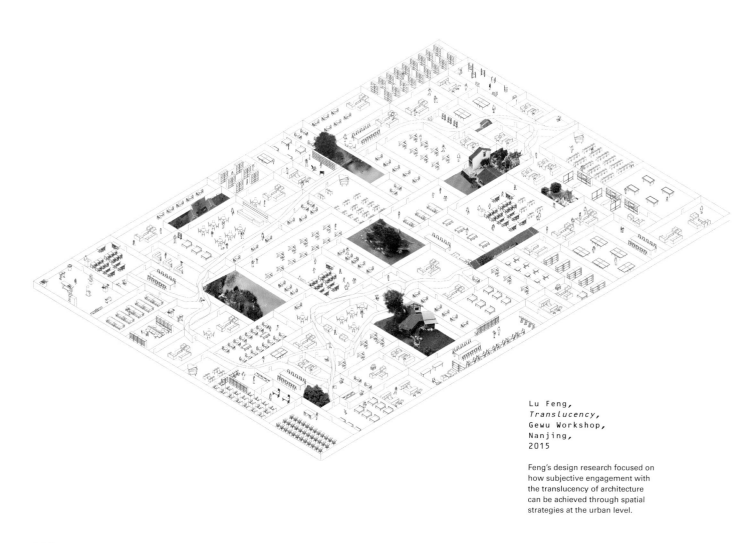

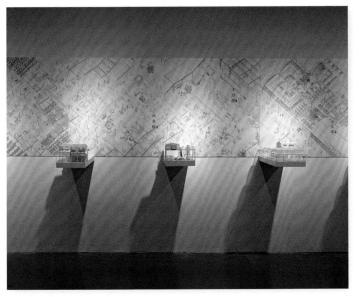

Bin Zhang,
Urban Farm Reclusion,
'Investigate It' exhibition,
OCT Contemporary Art Terminal –
OCAT Shanghai,
2016

Here the architect envisioned 12 ordinary scenes of a temporary urban farm as infill on the site.

Yimin Guo, an architectural theorist, adapted the Japanese architect Wajirō Kon's philosophy of *Modernology*[2] to examine Chinese urban conditions. He considered the Nanjing site as a fragmented landscape of residues of reality not yet completely destroyed or replaced, and developed a method to reveal the everyday connections between those fragments. With the help of a 'detective group' to search the site and observe how local residents' use of space changes in relation to changes to the space itself, various spatial units were then assembled into a larger architectural volume to study the collective form.

Architect and critic Lu Feng raised the concept of two-fold translucency, of surface and of folding, employing this as both a theoretical agenda and a working method. For *Translucency*, his team investigated four notable elements of the site – the city wall, Yu Garden, industrial buildings and residential blocks – and analysed how these urban elements became translucent through certain spatial strategies. He argued that translucent urbanism creates a sense of interiority that invokes a subject narrative experience.

Beyond the Workshop
The direct output of the workshop included 10 pamphlets to visually demonstrate each of the proposals, and in the spring of 2016 a synonymous exhibition was held at the OCT Contemporary Art Terminal – OCAT Shanghai, for which all the investigators were invited to refine and present their ideas as installations. The purpose of the workshop and subsequent exhibition, however, was not to promote individual investigators or to celebrate their findings, but to disseminate a responsive approach to the investigation of things. Today, as design practice becomes ever more specific and operational, individual investigations and reflective thinking are essential to extend architectural knowledge through responsive experimentation. ᴆ

Yimin Guo, *Modernology*,
Gewu Workshop,
Nanjing,
2015

Section from a Manga scroll documenting a 'jungle' of everydayness as observed from the viewpoint of Modernology – a homage to Japanese architect Wajirō Kon's graphics.

Notes
1. During the Confucian revival in the 11th and 12th centuries, philosophers Cheng Yi (1033–1107) and later Zhu Xi (1130–1200) proposed the investigation of things (*gewu*) for the extension of knowledge (*zhizhi*). They raised doubts about the appropriateness of focusing exclusively on the illumination of the mind in self-cultivation and insisted that ideas were derived from responses to the various phenomena we encounter.
2. Instead of focusing on architecture as a material structure, Wajirō Kon was interested in its relationship to everyday life and society. He developed Modernology as a method for the scientific analysis of material culture. See Wajirō Kon and Ignacio Adriasola, 'What Is Modernology' [1927], *Review of Japanese Culture and Society* 28, 2016, pp 62–73.

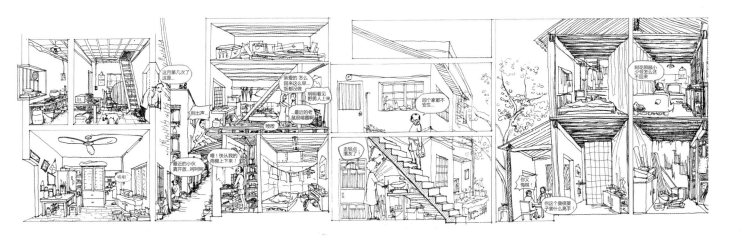

Amateur Architecture Studio,
Ningbo History Museum,
Ningbo,
Zhejiang province,
2008

The mountainous mass of the museum
is cleverly subverted by the irregular
prismatic geometry of its angular walls,
and by the delicate patterning of the
as-found masonry pieces that surface its
concrete structure.

Design Resea
in a Global

Murray Fraser

Turning
East

rch in China
Context

What are the defining qualities of China's current homegrown architectural pioneers, and how might they next evolve? **Murray Fraser**, Professor of Architecture and Global Culture and Vice-Dean of Research at the Bartlett School of Architecture, University College London, charts the background of design research from its Western roots, and investigates how recent generations of Chinese architects have been taking it in a new direction – from Wang Shu and Lu Wenyu's Amateur Architecture Studio to Atelier Deshaus, Atelier Archmixing and TAO (Trace Architecture Office).

Atelier Deshaus,
Long Museum West Bund,
Xuhui,
Shanghai,
2014

This partial view of the front elevation at dusk captures the museum's atmospheric qualities, with its generous public square in front and elegant vaults seeming to embrace the retained coal hoppers.

After a lengthy period in which seemingly the only new projects one ever heard about in China were those by international 'starchitects', the situation in recent years is greatly transformed. A very different type of building now features far higher on the radar, designed by innovative Chinese practices, and perhaps exemplified by Atelier Deshaus's Long Museum in the far West Bund of Shanghai, which opened in 2014. It is a brilliantly inventive piece of design, not least in retaining a landscape of old coal hoppers and loading cranes to offset its smooth, white intersecting vaulted ceilings.

Something else is particularly striking when visiting the Long Museum: here is a China of retrofit, not virgin urbanisation, and of carefully considered design, not lash-it-up-fast crudeness. What, then, had happened to the fabled speed and destructiveness of Chinese building production that Rem Koolhaas and others had been banging on about for years? For instance, in the *Harvard Design School Project on the City: Great Leap Forward* (2001), which highlighted the rapid development of the Pearl River Delta, Koolhaas claimed: 'A maelstrom of modernization is destroying everywhere the existing conditions in Asia and everywhere creating a new urban substance.'[1]

Of course, there had already been inklings of a change that was taking place in China. An exhibition in April 2012 at the Building Centre in Store Street, London, organised by *Urban Environment Design* magazine and titled 'From Beijing to London: Sixteen Contemporary Chinese Architects' (the opening of which was attended by many in the know, including the late Zaha Hadid) revealed glimpses of an up-and-coming generation of highly talented, highly educated younger Chinese architects. Hui Wang of URBANUS gave a fascinating introductory lecture. A new phase was clearly in gestation, with the *RIBA Journal* commenting: 'The message from the show … is that all Chinese architecture is not hell-for-leather urban development. There are many different and subtle sides to it.'[2]

This is precisely where this current △ issue fits in. Architectural practice in China is splintering and growing in diverse ways, and to those of us looking through Western-tinted spectacles, it is the intellectually engaged practitioners pursuing innovative avenues of design research that are leading the way. These younger Chinese architects are no longer hidebound by the restrictive practices of design institutes or large state departments, as has been pointed out recently by Charlie Xue and Guanghui Ding.[3] What, then, are the evolving principles and practices in China, and what might we expect to see in future?

Typical pattern of Shanghai's recent urban development, Huangpu, Shanghai, 2017

As in other Chinese cities, three levels of urbanism now prevail in the Huangpu district of Shanghai: low-rise dwellings in the foreground, mid-rise apartments and offices in Xiaodongmen behind, and the globally facing skyscrapers of Pudong across the Huangpu River.

A Brief Recap of Design Research in Architecture

Before looking at what is happening in China, it is worth recapping the idea of architectural design research. As a broad term, it refers to those particular forms of knowledge and insight that only those engaged in speculative design can produce – albeit always operating symbiotically and dialectically with other, more traditional methods of research.[4] Design research is open-ended, rigorous, lateral, iterative and creative, and as such cannot be conflated with scientific, historical, sociological or technological approaches.

While it can be argued that architects have engaged in 'design research' for a very long time – in the Western tradition, some say back to the Italian Renaissance, when *disegno* became an abstract intellectual conception distinct from the building trades – the first recorded use of the term I have found is in Eliel Saarinen's *The City: Its Growth, Its Decay, Its Future*, published in 1943 in America.[5] Clearly anticipating postwar reconstruction, and set within a climate of intense military research at a time when the secret 'Manhattan Project' to build the atomic bomb was underway, it identified an innovative 'two-fold movement' within design research. Saarinen's diagram showed, as one line along the bottom, the architect being engaged in conceiving specific buildings to create a new city, staggered in 10-year intervals over a period of 50 years. Along the top was another line, this time heading backwards from 50 years in the future to the present day. For Saarinen this represented the other part of design research, where architects are able to imagine a completed future city and then work out the steps needed to arrive at it. He thus argued that any act of design involved this two-fold movement: one projecting buildings into the future and the other analysing them as a mode of research, with the readjusted result being the city, or building, that was designed.

This was an astonishing formulation, yet one which Saarinen – originally an exponent of National Romanticism in his native Finland, before winning second place in the 1923 Chicago Tribune Tower competition, emigrating to the US, and designing notable structures such as the Kleinhans Concert Hall in Buffalo, New York, and the Cranbrook School of Design outside Detroit in Michigan (which he also ran) – could never implement. He died in 1950, by which point he was already being eclipsed by his more talented son, Eero Saarinen, who treated all of his projects, until his own untimely death in 1961, as original research investigations into new materials and technologies such as stainless steel, Corten steel, mirror glass, cable-slung tensile roofs and so on.

Design research developed hugely from the 1960s through seminal works such as Koolhaas's *Delirious New York* (1978), Bernard Tschumi's *Manhattan Transcripts* (1981), and the complete oeuvre of Lebbeus Woods, which in retrospect should not be treated merely as 'paper' architecture, but as a phenomenally intense and productive stream of innovative exploration. Today, many architects around the globe have seized the design research baton, a trend supported by PhD Design programmes at the Bartlett School of Architecture at University College London (UCL), RMIT University in Melbourne and elsewhere. It is a shift that has also been pursued by two waves of Chinese architects of slightly different generations.

Eliel Saarinen,
Design research diagram from *The City: Its Growth, Its Decay, Its Future*, 1943

Saarinen's inventive conception of design research in which the architect's idealised vision along the top row is modified by the various adjustments, as shown in time sequence along the bottom, needed to bring the design to fruition.

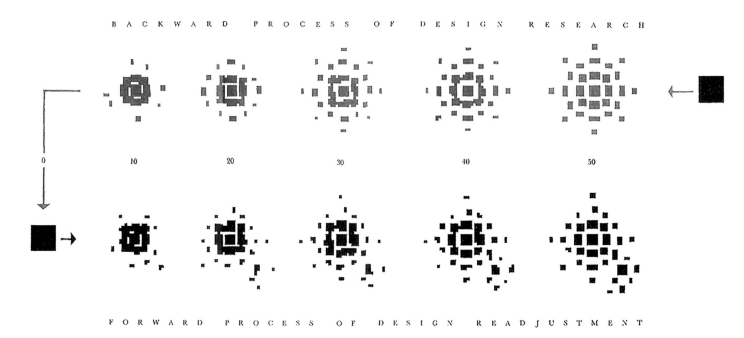

Their ongoing scheme for the Xiangshan Campus of the China Academy of Art, now with over 20 extremely different structures, has become a veritable showpiece, creating an array of buildings that mix functionally specific with unprogrammed spaces in a scintillating manner.

Amateur Architecture Studio,
Xiangshan Campus (Phase 2),
China Academy of Art,
Hangzhou,
Zhejiang province,
2007–

Construction of the university campus has been ongoing for almost two decades, and now includes some 25 structures. All are different, as seen in this refectory interior, its window arrangement having the feel of Chinese logogram characters.

Initial Changes in the Chinese Approach

The figures usually credited with forging a revitalised vision for Chinese modern architecture are those born during the 1960s who were able to study and work in Western countries – even becoming successful heads of architectural schools in the US, such as Qingyun Ma (University of Southern California/MADA spam) and Yung Ho Chang (Massachusetts Institute of Technology/Atelier FCJZ). China's growing wealth and power now positions it as the world's second largest economy, behind the US, and so perhaps an increasing awareness of Chinese architecture in North America was inevitable. Certainly many American firms like Skidmore, Owings & Merrill are operating extensively in China while also employing a good many Chinese graduates in their US offices.

However, the architects that probably did most to break the mould internationally – and who appear to suffer a lot of professional jealousy in China as a consequence – are the husband-and-wife team of Wang Shu and Lu Wenyu, following a very different route. Together they have practised in Hangzhou since 1997 under the banner of Amateur Architecture Studio, while also presiding over the architectural school at the China Academy of Art in Hangzhou. Wang Shu has bemoaned the fact that he usually gets singled out for attention without proper recognition given to Lu Wenyu – as when, in 2012, he became the first Chinese architect to be awarded the Pritzker Prize. Together, their ongoing scheme for the Xiangshan Campus of the China Academy of Art, now with over 20 extremely different structures, has become a veritable showpiece, creating an array of buildings that mix functionally specific with unprogrammed spaces in a scintillating manner.

The Amateur Architecture Studio project that most hit the button outside China, however, is the rock-like Ningbo History Museum, opened in 2008, which deploys the concept – originally termed *spolia*, referring to the reuse of Roman classical remains, and featured perhaps most stunningly in Jože Plečnik's National and University Library in 1930s Ljubljana – of recycling existing materials to construct the new. In this case the heterogeneous array of stones, bricks and tiles for its surfacing were collected from many local sources. Elsewhere on the museum's facade, concrete-cased bamboo is used, referencing another traditional Chinese building method.

The result is a patterned masonry structure that speaks poignantly of the new China struggling with how to deal with its older ways of life, and seeking to fuse past and future together. The sheer massiveness of the museum, and the apparently random aesthetic of its asymmetrical forms and materials, makes it a badge that begins to speak critically of recent socioeconomic transformations in China, particularly of what thoughtless commercial architecture has inflicted. As Wang Shu argues, 'we must not demolish history in order to develop'.[6]

Atelier Archmixing,
Xishi Grand Theatre,
Zhuji,
Zhejiang province,
2017

The sinuous protective ring around the theatre auditorium is cleverly left open in certain parts and made solid in others, enabling views through the structure while providing sufficient enclosure to form a courtyard for open-air film screenings and other events.

A Further Step-Change

Yet the work of Wang Shu and Lu Wenyu still represents an older continuity that is rooted in the Chinese academies. Today a fresher and younger generation – those born from the 1970s onwards – is introducing a different sense of energy, again with an eye on architecture in the West and elsewhere, but with its own particular marks.

The aforementioned practice of Atelier Deshaus in Shanghai (see their article on pp 88–93) is an interesting node among this new generation. Founded in 2001 by three young talents – Yichun Liu, Yifeng Chen and Shen Zhuang – the former pair have continued to run the practice since Zhuang left in 2009 to set up Atelier Archmixing, another of the contributors to this issue of *D* (see pp 52–7).

In the case of Atelier Deshaus, the Long Museum West Bund in Shanghai demonstrates well the types of design research the practice is engaged in. Although the actual finished construction is a bit rough – one can only imagine if Japanese or Swiss contractors had been able to cast those ambitious vaults – the sense of volumetric and visual interconnection as one walks around points to the sheer amount of modelling and testing that went into the design. The final effect is memorable, mixing rugged industrial steel with the smooth concrete, plaster and glass of the new insertions. Sitting within its new park, the Long Museum offers generous public space exemplified on the riverfront by reusing some of the old crane towers, animating that space through public inhabitation.

The sense of volumetric and visual interconnection as one walks around points to the sheer amount of modelling and testing that went into the design. The final effect is memorable, mixing rugged industrial steel with the smooth concrete, plaster and glass of the new insertions.

As in effect a splinter from Atelier Deshaus, Atelier Archmixing is another practice now pursuing closely observed design research into urban contexts alongside formally and structurally innovative schemes. Among the latter projects is the Xishi Grand Theatre in Zhuji, Zhejiang province, completed in 2017, in which a larger and lower outer ring around an elliptical auditorium creates a curving courtyard that is to be used for outdoor film screenings and similar events. Other Chinese practices, many included in this *D*, could equally be cited.

Atelier Deshaus,
Long Museum West Bund,
Xuhui,
Shanghai,
2014

In this worm's-eye axonometric that seems more complex than it is, the intersecting nature of the museum's (partial) concrete vaults, often set at right-angles to each other, is projected particularly vividly.

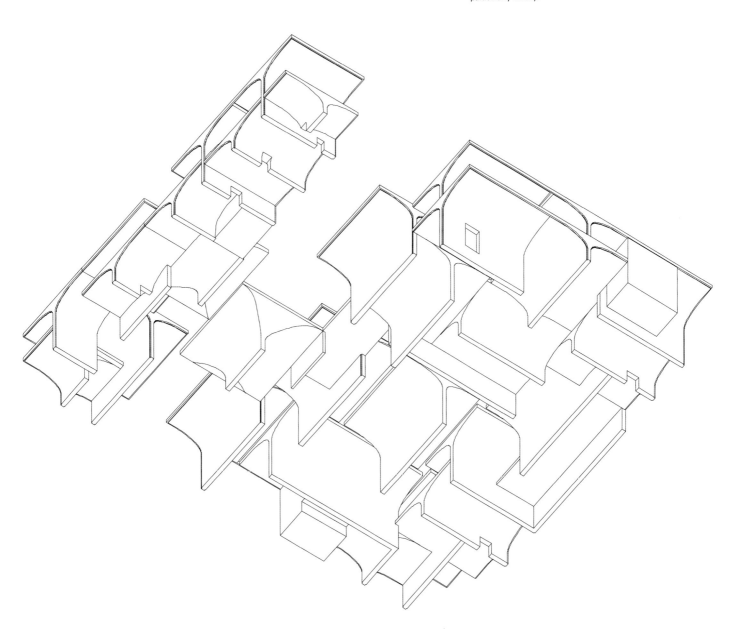

One firm that is pursuing fascinating lines of research investigation that are less about urbanism and more about materiality, is TAO (Trace Architecture Office), which was formed in 2009. Founder and principal architect Li Hua's approach involves looking carefully at the conditions and traditions of the places they are designing for. An excellent example is the practice's Xinzhai Coffee Manor near Baoshan in Yunnan province – a highland subtropical region close to the border with Myanmar that now grows prized Arabica coffee. Unlike in most of China, where traditional architecture is timber framed, here a heritage of brick construction is invoked in its serene cross-vaults. There are nods also to Western brick architecture, with a notably strong influence from Rafael Moneo's 1986 scheme for the National Museum of Roman Art in Mérida, Spain.

TAO (Trace Architecture Office),
Xinzhai Coffee Manor,
Lujiangba,
Baoshan,
Yunnan province,
2016

TAO's emphasis on constructional logic was pursued rigorously through full-scale test prototypes that informed the eventual erection of the repeated brick cross-vaults. The result is a rhythmic and elegant formal solution that manages to balance indigenous craft techniques with contemporary research.

Unlike in most of China, where traditional architecture is timber framed, here a heritage of brick construction is invoked in its serene cross-vaults.

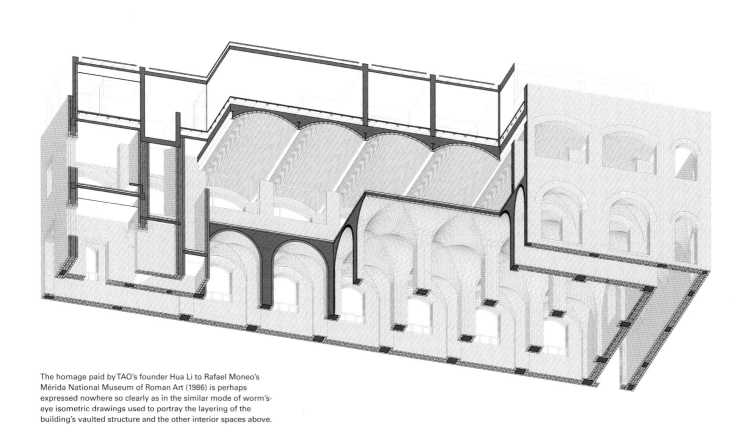

The homage paid by TAO's founder Hua Li to Rafael Moneo's Mérida National Museum of Roman Art (1986) is perhaps expressed nowhere so clearly as in the similar mode of worm's-eye isometric drawings used to portray the layering of the building's vaulted structure and the other interior spaces above.

Urban street systems,
Huangpu,
Shanghai,
2014

Overlapping networks in the ordinary domestic areas of Chinese cities revolve around daily necessities such as clothes drying, electrical supplies and air-conditioning units, and create an elegantly ephemeral aesthetic. This kind of anonymous urban condition underpins much of the design research by younger Chinese firms.

Fertile Ground

What is inherently different about the design research being carried out by this younger Chinese generation? In Europe, design research frequently tends to revolve around some form of relationship to past traditions, whether from the Renaissance, Neoclassicism or Modernism. In the US this appears particularly fixated on the impact of digitalisation. In China, with its very different lineage, these historical and technological references are more general and diffuse: instead the concern is more about dealing with the exigencies of the present, both in addressing the ultra-rapid rates of urbanisation and modernisation, and, from that analysis, anticipating future needs and directions. While design research in Western countries often involves speculations and representations of alternative worlds, as critiques of the status quo, in China there seems an acceptance of the task of conceiving new possibilities from within the existing socioeconomic conditions.

One gets the sense that having transformed their mode of practice this much, and now with the bit between their teeth, Chinese architects are likely to be setting the pace in design research in the coming decades. With much of the country's urban development still to happen, the act of breaking away from soulless generic, energy-guzzling buildings would be a godsend not only for Chinese citizens, but also for the environmental and ecological health of the planet. Smarter, lower-energy and reduced-carbon developments is the goal of this new trend towards architectural design research in China. No one can predict where exactly things will head, but Chinese architecture will certainly be one of the most fertile grounds for thinking and practice for the foreseeable future. ⌀

Notes
1. Rem Koolhaas, 'Introduction: City of Exacerbated Difference', in Judy Chuihua Chung et al (eds), Harvard Design School Project on the City 1: Great Leap Forward, Taschen (Cologne), 2001, p 27.
2. Hugh Pearman, 'China Syndrome', RIBA Journal, 18 April 2012: www.ribaj.com/culture/china-syndrome.
3. Charlie QL Xue and Guanghui Ding, A History of Design Institutes in China: From Mao to Market, Routledge (London), 2018.
4. Murray Fraser (ed), Design Research in Architecture: An Overview, Ashgate (Farnham, UK), 2013.
5. Eliel Saarinen, The City: Its Growth, Its Decay, Its Future, Reinhold Publishing (New York), 1943, pp 370–77.
6. Quoted in Amy Frearson, 'Key Projects by Wang Shu', Dezeen, 28 February 2012: www.dezeen.com/2012/02/28/key-projects-by-wang-shu/.

No one can predict where exactly things will head, but Chinese architecture will certainly be one of the most fertile grounds for thinking and practice for the foreseeable future.

Alternative Modernity, Rural Rediscovery and What Next

The Ongoing Debate on the Modern in China

While modernity in the West is seen as essentially related to urbanisation, in China it has long been recognised that cities are not the sole location for cultural and technological innovation. After summarising the philosophical factors that led to this more nuanced state of affairs, **Li Zhang**, Professor of Architecture and Associate Dean of the School of Architecture at Tsinghua University and leader of Beijing design office TeamMinus, identifies three modes of modernity that have coexisted in China over the last three decades – one of which is exclusively rural.

Over the last three decades the breakneck speed of urbanisation in China has transformed it into an architectural melting pot. This has had far-reaching consequences, challenging the magnitude of late 20th-century Chinese Modernist technocracy, which built upon short-lived Congrès Internationaux d'Architecture Moderne (CIAM) beliefs,[1] while also triggering a plethora of cynical and backward-looking commentaries.[2] The ubiquitous bigness and newness of Chinese new towns, which are overwhelmingly associated with an equally ubiquitous ugliness, has proved an underlying trajectory for these theories of anxious or desperate modernity. This issue of D, in its keenness to identify traces of independent experimentation and research, can be viewed if not as a retaliation, at least as an effective response to these negative theories – regardless of how few and far between this experimental work is in the vast standardised Chinese urban landscape.

A typical Kuhnian paradigm is playing out in the background here,[3] the underlying assumption being that cities are the primary site of intellectual exploration. In Europe this might be true. In China, however, there is a 2,000-year history that suggests it is probably not the case. Over two millennia of pre-modern civilisation in China, the dialectic between Confucianism and Taoism was the main cultural engine.[4] While Confucianism provided the pillar for grand imperial spectacle and institutional interactions in urban life, Taoism sheltered private escapes and inquiries in a sub-urban and rural context. It was only when traditional Chinese intellectuals were outside the political and social confines of the city that they were most free to explore and to experiment. So much so that all the way up to the brink of modernity, in the mid- to late 17th century, Chinese art and architecture enjoyed a brief period of extreme self-consciousness and autonomy in places far away from power centres. It bore all the necessary characteristics of a home-grown modernity, the phenomenon referred to by some as 'alternative modernity'.[5] Painters like Shi Tao in the late 17th century adventured in new brush strokes and multipoint perspectives that completely deconstructed Song dynasty landscape painting traditions. Entrepreneurs in the early 18th century experimented with juxtaposition and hybridisation, for example Zhang Ze in his private rural retreat in Yuyao, Zheijang province (c 1740), which collages materials he imported from overseas with components from his home village. Craftsmen like those in Gaoping took great pleasure in making radical mud sculptures capitalising on the unique technique of iron-thread wireframes.

Shi Tao,
Scenes Inspired by a Tao Yuanming Poem,
1690s

It was his political despair (being a royal descendent of the previous dynasty) that freed landscape painter Shi Tao (1642–1707) from China's urban power struggles and the conservative artistic approaches of Confucianism. In this painting series he brings the idyllic escape by the poet Tao Yuanming to life.

As enlightening and inspiring, or even shocking as these early traces of alternative modernity were, they were interrupted when the Manchu dynasty (which was developing along a very different cultural path) conquered Beijing and Imperial China in 1644, and then again by the waves of invasion by European colonialists in the 19th century. After that, for over a century, from the 1840s through to the 1950s, Chinese art and architecture were practically a ground of imported ideas with one major source of influence being replaced by another: first the Catholic Europeans, then the Protestant Americans, then the Soviet Russians.

The Great Reform that has been taking place since the late 1970s has not only created economic booms, but also brought back the unresolved debate on Chinese modernity in art and architecture, along with the growing middle class and the expansion of intellectual curiosity. Three decades of rapid urbanisation can not only be seen as an accumulation of built stuff, but also be read as passages of arguments in the modernity debate. It is not as black and white as generic ugliness versus acupuncture beauty. It is shaded, intertwined, multi-threaded and multilayered, registering both poignance and optimism.

We have to paint with a broad brush here if we dare to draw one big picture. Three modes, or three interpretations of modernity, can be found in Chinese architecture over the last 30 years. Two are primarily anchored in cities: 'received modernity' and 'reflective modernity'. One is solely rural, as it was four centuries ago: 'alternative modernity'.

Received Modernity

Received modernity is the most apparent of the three modes. It is the continued adoption of imported ideas, mostly from the US and Western Europe. These ideas, however, do not necessarily represent the best from the developed world. Far from it. They are what an arcade elicits from a flâneur:[6] consumerism, technocracy and iconography. They are particularly prevalent among Chinese urban developments built between the 1980s and early 2000s. RTKL's New Dongan Market, for example, completed in 1996 in Beijing, is notoriously ruthless in eliminating local memories. The poor performance of Mario Cucinella's Sino-Italian Ecological and Energy Efficient Building (also in Beijing) in 2007 raises great scepticism of the high-cost technological solutions. The fire in OMA's incomplete Beijing Television Cultural Centre in 2009, which was caused by an illegal Chinese New Year firework display arrogantly authorised by the China Central Television (CCTV) company without the required permit from local government and despite repeated police warnings, shocked all Beijingers, placing a huge question mark over iconic buildings regarded as incarnations of superheroes.

RTKL,
New Dongan Market,
Wangfujing,
Beijing,
1997

In the 1990s, American consumerism in China was seen as 'progress', represented here in RTKL's 100,000-square-metre (1.1 million-square-foot) shopping mall adorned with Postmodern symbols in an attempt to pay tribute to the traditional market and community it replaced. Projects like this usually eliminate entire neighbourhoods and their memories.

TeamMinus,
Jinchang Culture Centre,
Jinchang,
Gansu province,
2013

Inspired by its desert mountain surroundings, the centre's southwest-facing zigzagged facade along the main concourse creates a warm, interior public space, giving this previously featureless mining city a long-awaited identity.

Reflective Modernity

The problems incurred by received modernity are intrinsic to an approach that simply reproduces ideas and models regardless of cultural, social or local setting. Disregarding the particularities of communities and places can have disastrous consequences. Reflective modernity tries to tackle this. Since the late 1990s, reflective modernity has been a course shared by many Chinese architects engaged in advancing a critical urban argument. Human scale, identity, cultural continuity and social cohesion are among the most usual aspects addressed. Scenic Architecture Office's Huaxin Pavilion (2013) dematerialises itself in the exuberance of a Shanghai park, delivering sheer navigational fun for the local inhabitants. TeamMinus's Jinchang Culture Centre (2013) in Gansu province bestows a long-awaited identity, unmistakably reminiscent of the local mountains, on a featureless mining city in the Chinese northwest desert. OPEN Architecture's Workers' Dormitory (2012) in Fujian province provides those working on the video-game production line with an easy and relaxed collective home, along with a great sense of belonging.

Scenic Architecture
Office,
Huaxin Pavilion,
Shanghai,
2013

Dematerialised, multifaceted and playful, this lovely little structure launches an attack on the spectacularity and monumentality of Chinese public spaces.

Chen Haoru,
Taiyang Commune Farm Buildings,
Linan,
Zhejiang province,
2013

Chen Haoru's Taiyang Farm Buildings adopt a common bamboo structural solution to deliver harmony across species, providing pleasant spaces for farmers, pigs and chickens alike.

OPEN Architecture,
Workers' Dormitory,
Xiamen,
Fujian province,
2012

Continuing the office's preoccupation with social equality in China, the Workers' Dormitory advocates a new model for raising the quality of accommodation for the modern workforce. Its semi-closed multistorey courtyard is safe, light and provides a sense of belonging.

Alternative Modernity

If reflective modernity gives thoughtful critiques on the blindness of received modernity, alternative modernity goes even further. Suspending the domination of cities, it goes back deep into rural China to explore the scenarios of homegrown modernity once again emerging from there. It endorses the claim that in China good cities cannot exist without a good countryside. By again taking up the Confucianism–Taoism dialectic it argues that rural areas can genuinely be a field of both technological and cultural innovation.

Such an argument is of course a contentious one. And making it all the more contentious is the recent trend of contemporary Chinese architects rushing into the rural area, one after another.

Chen Haoru's Taiyang Commune Farm Buildings (2013) in Linan, Zhejiang province, are a usual series of rural facilities that apply one basic structural solution to buildings of all programmes. Here, a cross-shaped modular unit, achieved through binding local bamboo sticks, is the form-giver. A feature of both the livestock areas and the farmers' tea pavilion, it creates a connection across co-living species. It is a silent and harmonious interpretation of an old Chinese belief, which has its origins in the 2nd century BC, that regards all things (and animals and humans) living in one area as intrinsically connected and mutually transferable.

It is a silent and harmonious interpretation of an old Chinese belief, which has its origins in the 2nd century BC, that regards all things (and animals and humans) living in one area as intrinsically connected and mutually transferable.

dEEP Architects,
Hostel for Volunteers,
Niubei Mountain,
Yaan,
Sichuan province,
2015

The architects' clever treatment, inserting a modern timber structure in this traditional vernacular house, not only provides additional space for visiting volunteers, but also a dramatic reshaping of the traditional tiled roof that had never previously been achieved.

dEEP Architects' Hostel for Volunteers (2015) in a remote mountain village in Sichuan is another example of being rural and modern at the same time. The hostel is an innovative renovation of a dilapidated building. By using a parametric timber structure, and joining the structure with traditional roof tiles, the building achieves a delightful dialogue between new and old, and forms a distinctive yet amiable part of the village. The interior also reflects the same playfulness between new and old, featuring a modern repetitive modular plan and traditional fibres as partitions.

TeamMinus's Jianamani Visitor Centre (2013) in the Tibetan village of Yushu is an example of materiality under the guidance of spirituality. Being the visitor centre to the world's largest Tibetan Buddhist stone pile, it features 11 lookouts to the surrounding historic sites. The plan is a Tibetan square yard with a series of lookout decks rotating around it. The building uses masonry of local stone, recycled local wood components, and a traditional technique of heating using dried cow droppings. It is the explicit links with history and material continuity that make it a worthy case of the contemporary vernacular.

In DnA's Brown Sugar Factory in Songyang (2016) (see p 102–5 of this issue), what the female architect Tiantian Xu dares to do that few others have done is develop a programme-driven approach that optimises on the health and wellbeing of the building's users. The form of the factory's fabric, shared by both the workshop's volumes and the adjacent farmland, also derives from an intentional design effort. Light is taken in, and fumes are guided out easily by the unapologetic height of the main structures. Lower volumes, rendered in warmer and softer materials, provide convenient spaces that are usually unachievable in rural factories. DnA's unapologetic diagrammatic approach makes a convincing case here. Another unique character of the project is that it is completely supported by the local county government. The trajectory of Taoism shedding some light back onto Confucianism is intriguing.

So if alternative modernity fares so well in the Chinese countryside, effectively generating a movement independent of the other two modes of urban modernity, can it eventually find a way back into the cities and cause a bigger, wider movement? In his military theory, the great revolutionary hero of modern China, Chairman Mao, has written about the irregular form of warfare in which small groups of combatants defeat a larger and less mobile formal army.[7] If we are allowed to draw a wild analogy here, then the good things happening in the countryside at the small scale can and will influence the massive urban discourse. ⌂

Notes
1. Eric Mumford, *The CIAM Discourse on Urbanism, 1928–1960*, MIT Press (Cambridge, MA), 2002.
2. Chuihua Judy Chung *et al*, *Great Leap Forward / Harvard Design School Project on the City*, Taschen (Boston, MA), 2002.
3. Thomas Kuhn, *The Structure of Scientific Revolution*, University of Chicago Press (Chicago, IL), 1962.
4. Mu Qian, *Zhong Guo Wen Hua Shi Dao Lun (A Brief History of Chinese Civilisation)*, Shang Wu Yin Shu Guan (Beijing), 1947.
5. Jonathan Hay, *Shitao: Painting and Modernity in Early Qing China*, Cambridge University Press (Cambridge), 2001.
6. Susan Buck-Morss, *The Dialectics of Seeing: Walter Benjamin and the Arcades Project*, MIT Press (Cambridge, MA). 1991.
7. Mao Zedong, *Lun Chi Jiu Zhan (On Guerrilla Warfare)*, Ren Min Chu Ban She (Beijing), 1938 (English trans 1950).

TeamMinus,
Jianamani Visitor Centre,
Yushu,
Qinghai province,
2013

Its unique location and the story behind the world's largest Tibetan Buddhist stone pile for which it is the visitor centre are used here to make explicit the connections between the building and its surrounding historic sites.

CONTRIBUTORS

Lu Feng is an architect, researcher and curator. He received his PhD from the University of Sheffield in 2008, and is the founder of Shanghai-based Wuyang Architecture, which focuses on design practice with theoretical and critical thinking on architecture and urbanism. He was an adjunct professor at Nanjing University from 2009 to 2015, and is currently teaching an urban research and design course at Shanghai Jiaotong University.

Murray Fraser is Professor of Architecture and Global Culture, as well as Vice-Dean of Research, at the Bartlett School of Architecture, University College London (UCL). He has published extensively on design, architectural history and theory, urbanism, post-colonialism and cultural studies, including the edited book *Design Research in Architecture* (Routledge, 2013). He co-created the online Archigram Archival Project, and has won several awards for his work with the Palestine Regeneration Team. He is currently General Editor for the 21st edition of *Sir Banister Fletcher's Global History of Architecture*.

Xiao Fu is a registered architect and professor at the School of Architecture and Urban Planning, Nanjing University, where he is lead architect of the Integrated Architecture Studio. His main research interest is green building design methods and construction-based on building information modelling (BIM) technology. He is currently working as a subtask leader on the key research and development programme Green Building Systems Based on Chinese Culture in Developed Areas (2017YFC0702502).

Xiahong Hua is an associate professor at the College of Architecture and Urban Planning, Tongji University, and a visiting fellow at the School of Architecture, Yale University. She is an Architectural Criticism Committee Member of the Architectural Society of China, part-time Editor of *Time + Architecture* and Academic Advisor at Atelier Archmixing. A registered architect, architectural historian and theorist, her academic interests include the history of contemporary Chinese architecture, everyday urbanism and related design strategies, and architecture in consumer culture.

Qiuye Jin is a member of the Architectural Society of China, a professor at Beijing University of Civil Engineering and Architecture, co-founder of the Arcadia academic group, and an architecture critic. His fields of research include the translation of Chinese traditional design language into modern architecture and contemporary architectural thought in China. He is the author of the critical essay collection *Utopia on the Drawing Board* (2013). He received his PhD from Tsinghua University, Beijing, and MArch from Dalian University of Technology in Liaoning province.

Xinggang Li received his Doctor of Engineering degree from Tianjin University, where he is currently a visiting professor, and founded the Atelier Li Xinggang in 2003. He is also a design tutor at the School of Architecture, Tsinghua University. His architectural practice and research focus on integrating the idea of 'poetic scenery' and geometry. His practice has been honoured with design awards including the WA Chinese Architecture Awards (2014 and 2016) and ArchDaily Building of the Year Award (2018). He is also the recipient of the China Youth Science and Technology Award (2007) and the esteemed National Engineering Survey and Design Master Award (2016).

Yichun Liu graduated from Tongji University in Shanghai with a Bachelor of Architecture degree in 1991, and received his Master of Architecture in 1997. He is the partner and principal architect of Atelier Deshaus, which he co-founded with Shen Zhuang and Yifeng Chen in 2001. He is a guest professor at the College of Architecture and Urban Planning at Tongji and at the School of Architecture, Southeast University, Nanjing. He is an editorial advisory board member of the journals *The Architect* and *Architectural Journal China*.

James Shen received his MArch from the Massachusetts Institute of Technology (MIT) and a BSc in product design from California State University, Long Beach. He is a visiting lecturer at MIT and a Harvard Loeb Fellow. In 2010, he co-founded Beijing-based People's Architecture Office (PAO), a multidisciplinary studio focusing on social impact through design. The studio's award-winning works have been exhibited at the Venice Architecture Biennale, Harvard Graduate School of Design (GSD) and the London Design Museum. It was named an *Architectural Review* Emerging Architecture practice in 2017, and one of the world's five most innovative architecture offices by Fast Company in 2018.

Yehao Song is the Director of the Institute for Architecture and Technology Studies (IATS) at the School of Architecture, Tsinghua University, and Architect in Chief of SUP Atelier. His research focuses on sustainable design and theory in the fields of both architecture and urban design, while promoting the combination of modern design and vernacular architecture in China. His recent works and projects have won many national and international awards. He has also published many academic papers in both Chinese and international journals.

Hui Wang is a co-founder of URBANUS, based in Beijing and Shenzhen. Recognised as one of the leading firms in the new wave of Chinese design, the practice is committed to the Modernist belief that architecture is the pivotal force for a better society, and acts as a think-tank providing strategies for urbanism and architecture in the new millennium. Besides many of his social engagements, Wang is also a council member of the Architectural Society of China, and teaches part-time at Tsinghua University. His recent projects include the Botanical Conservatory for the 2019 Beijing International Horticulture Expo.

Shuo Wang is an architect, researcher and curator based in Beijing, and a founding principal of META-Project. He received his BArch from Tsinghua University and MArch from Rice University in Houston, Texas. He has worked for OMA on various large-scale projects in the UK, UAE and major Southeast Asian cities. He has also initiated a series of urban research projects via the META-Research parallel platform and is extending the idea across multiple contemporary media. In 2015, a new component, META-Prototype, was integrated into the practice.

Xiang Wang is a post-doctoral researcher at Tongji University where he leads the Digital Design Research Center (DDRC) with Philip F Yuan. Through this and his work at Archi-Union Architects, he demonstrates the possibilities of applying new fabrication techniques to multiple traditional materials and the potential of creating a brand-new architectural expression.

Xin Wang is an associate professor at the School of Architecture of the China Academy of Art in Hangzhou, leads the Zaoyuan Gardening Studio practice, and is a co-founder of the academic group Arcadia, which is dedicated to contemporary experimentation in Chinese gardens, as well as Editor-in-Chief of its eponymous journal. Zaoyuan Garden Studio's projects include the Red Pavilion in the Silk Road Art Park, Quanzhou, Fujian province (2015), and 'Tea Party under the Pine Shade', Zhang village, Anji county, Zhejiang province (2016).

Wei You is an assistant researcher and architect at the School of Architecture and Urban Planning, Nanjing University. His research interests include analysis and evaluation of building energy consumption and the physical environment, and passive green building design. He was also a principal investigator for the China National Natural Science Foundation grant 'Research on the Optimization of the Texture of Residential Area Based on the Assessment of Building Natural Ventilation Potential'.

Philip F Yuan is the founder of Shanghai-based Archi-Union Architects and a professor at Tongji University. His research and design in China involves the application of prototypical methods and advanced manufacturing techniques, and focuses on how digital tools offer the possibility of a new authorship for today's architects based on an understanding of culture, materials and the built environment.

Li Zhang is a professor of architecture and Associate Dean of the School of Architecture, Tsinghua University. He leads the design office Atelier TeamMinus in Beijing. He is a standing board member of the Architectural Society of China and the Editor-in-Chief of the Chinese magazine *World Architecture*. His field of interest is pre-industrial oriental philosophy and its contemporary interpretation. He focuses his design and research on the relationship between space and the human body. Atelier TeamMinus won the Zumtobel Group Award for Young Practice in 2017 and has also received numerous national awards.

Xin Zhang is an associate professor at the School of Architecture, Tsinghua University, where he currently teaches the Architectural Design Studio and Architectural Lighting (graduate and undergraduate level) courses. He began lighting design practice in 2006, and the lighting concepts of his design studio are now finding applications in a much broader field. During 2012–13 he was a visiting scholar at the Martin Centre for Architectural and Urban Studies at the University of Cambridge.

Jingxiang Zhu is an associate professor at the School of Architecture, Chinese University of Hong Kong (CUHK). He studied at Southeast University and ETH Zurich. Before joining CUHK in 2004 he taught at Southeast University and Nanjing University, and practised as an architect in mainland China for 10 years. His research focuses on the new articulation of structures and space, lightweight building systems, cost-effective architecture and vernacular construction. His innovative prefab systems have been adopted in both earthquake-stricken and developing areas. He is the recipient of several Chinese academic awards, as well as the *Wall Street Journal* China Innovator of the Year Award (2012) and Hong Kong Construction Council Innovation Award (2015).

Shen Zhuang is co-founder and principal architect of Atelier Archmixing, and a guest professor at the College of Architecture and Urban Planning, Tongji University. A pioneering young Chinese architect, he was the recipient of the Young Explorer Award at the Chinese Architecture Media Awards (CAMA) in 2016. He has participated in group exhibitions including: 'How about China?' at the Centre Pompidou, Paris (2003); 'Contemporary China' at the NAI, Rotterdam (2006); and 'Towards A Critical Pragmatism: Contemporary Architecture in China' at Harvard GSD (2016). His work has also been published in *Architecture Research Quarterly, Architectural Record, Domus, A+U, Perspecta* and the *Architectural Journal*.

What is *Architectural Design*?

Founded in 1930, *Architectural Design* (△) is an influential and prestigious publication. It combines the currency and topicality of a newsstand journal with the rigour and production qualities of a book. With an almost unrivalled reputation worldwide, it is consistently at the forefront of cultural thought and design.

Each title of △ is edited by an invited Guest-Editor, who is an international expert in the field. Renowned for being at the leading edge of design and new technologies, △ also covers themes as diverse as architectural history, the environment, interior design, landscape architecture and urban design.

Provocative and pioneering, △ inspires theoretical, creative and technological advances. It questions the outcome of technical innovations as well as the far-reaching social, cultural and environmental challenges that present themselves today.

For further information on △, subscriptions and purchasing single issues see:

http://onlinelibrary.wiley.com/journal/10.1002/%28ISSN%291554-2769

Volume 87 No 6
ISBN 978 1119 340188

Volume 88 No 1
ISBN 978 1119 379515

Volume 88 No 2
ISBN 978 1119 254416

Volume 88 No 3
ISBN 978 1119 332633

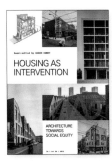

Volume 88 No 4
ISBN 978 1119 337843

Volume 88 No 5
ISBN 978 1119 328148

How to Subscribe
With 6 issues a year, you can subscribe to △ (either print, online or through the △ App for iPad)

Institutional subscription
£310 / $580
print or online

Institutional subscription
£388 / $725
combined print and online

Personal-rate subscription
£136 / $215
print and iPad access

Student-rate subscription
£90 / $137
print only

△ App for iPad
6-issue subscription:
£44.99 / US$64.99
Individual issue:
£9.99 / US$13.99

To subscribe to print or online
E: cs-journals@wiley.com

Americas
E: cs-journals@wiley.com
T: +1 781 388 8598
or +1 800 835 6770
(toll free in the USA & Canada)

Europe, Middle East and Africa
E: cs-journals@wiley.com
T: +44 (0) 1865 778315

Asia Pacific
E: cs-journals@wiley.com
T: +65 6511 8000

Japan (for Japanese-speaking support)
E: cs-japan@wiley.com
T: +65 6511 8010
or 005 316 50 480
(toll-free)

Visit our Online Customer Help available in 7 languages at www.wileycustomerhelp.com/ask